AMAZING S

THE
FAMOUS FIVE

Canada's Crusaders for Women's Rights

BARBARA SMITH

VICTORIA · VANCOUVER · CALGARY

For my great-granddaughter,
Cait Deborah Marie

Copyright © 2019 Barbara Smith

All rights reserved. No part of this publication may be reproduced, stored in a retrieval system, or transmitted in any form or by any means—electronic, mechanical, audio recording, or otherwise—without the written permission of the publisher or a licence from Access Copyright, Toronto, Canada.

Heritage House Publishing Company Ltd.
heritagehouse.ca

Cataloguing information available from Library
and Archives Canada

978-1-77203-233-8 (pbk)
978-1-77203-234-5 (epub)

Edited by Audrey McClellan
Proofread by Stephen Harries
Cover images L–R: Louise McKinney, GA: NA 5395-5; Irene Parlby, GA: NA 2204-12; Emily Murphy, PAA: A3355; Henrietta Edwards, GA: NA 2607-7; and Nellie McClung, SA 1981-023-004A

The interior of this book was produced on 100% post-consumer recycled paper, processed chlorine free, and printed with vegetable-based inks.

We acknowledge the financial support of the Government of Canada through the Canada Book Fund (CBF) and the Canada Council for the Arts, and the Province of British Columbia through the British Columbia Arts Council and the Book Publishing Tax Credit.

23 22 21 20 19 1 2 3 4 5

Printed in Canada

Contents

Never retract, never explain, never apologize:
just get the thing done and let them howl.

NELLIE MCCLUNG
a proud member of the Famous Five

Prologue

EARLY IN THE afternoon of Saturday, August 27, 1927, Emily Murphy was busy preparing to receive visitors. Four of her most respected friends would be joining her to enjoy tea and slices of date and nut loaf on the front porch of her home on Edmonton's south side.

She had chosen her clothes carefully, knowing that her friends would have as well. All of them would want to show every respect for the importance of their mission that afternoon. Emily also knew that each of her friends would be wearing a hat, while the etiquette of the day dictated that she, in her own home, would not.

Of course, Emily Murphy had hosted many gatherings that were larger and more formal than this one, but she knew today's gathering held considerable significance. These friends were all accomplished women who knew and admired one another, and the five shared an important common purpose. Henrietta Muir Edwards was a social activist, a reformer, and a legal expert. Nellie McClung was an internationally respected author and speaker, who had been a key figure in winning the vote for Western Canadian women. Louise McKinney was one of the first two women elected to a Canadian legislature and was president of the powerful Women's Christian Temperance Union in Canada. Irene Parlby was a member of Alberta's legislative assembly and by 1927 had served as minister without portfolio for six years, tirelessly fighting for the law's protection of women and children.

This short guest list had been chosen with great care. Emily could have called on her husband, one of her daughters, a neighbour and a colleague, all of whom would have fulfilled the requirement of being "interested parties," but the occasion called for as substantial an impact as possible. And for that, Emily Murphy knew exactly who to choose. Individually, each one of these women was strong, determined, and intelligent. Collectively, they were a force to be reckoned with, and Emily realized she would need that sort of support because this was a battle that would likely become contentious.

Later that afternoon, when all five women were settled into wicker chairs on the screened-in sunporch, Murphy showed her friends a letter she had written to the Governor General in which she asked two questions of critical importance to all Canadian women. Her guests were not surprised. They all knew the purpose of this get-together was not merely social. After they had each read the letter, they nodded in agreement and, in alphabetical order, signed their names.

Prologue

Years later, Nellie McClung recalled the occasion and wrote, "It was a perfect day in harvest time. Blue haze lay on the horizon. Wheat fields, now dotted with stooks, were waiting for the threshing machine. Bees droned in the delphiniums and roses. We sat on her verandah and talked the afternoon away. Then we put our names to the petition and it was sent to Ottawa."[1]

And with this action, the long slow process that would see Canadian women finally legally recognized as "persons" was set in motion.

Emily Murphy's Recipe for Date and Nut Loaf

Emily Murphy rarely spent time preparing food, but on August 27, 1927, she may have baked her popular date and nut loaf to serve to Henrietta Edwards, Nellie McClung, Louise McKinney, and Irene Parlby before they all signed the letter that began the process that would become known as the Persons Case.[2]

4 cups of flour
4 teaspoons of baking powder
1 cup of white sugar
1 cup of chopped walnuts
1 cup of chopped dates
1 egg, well beaten
2 cups of sweet milk
Pinch of salt

Let rise 20 minutes. Bake 1 to 1½ hours slowly. Makes two loaves. For one loaf use half the amounts and bake for ¾ of an hour.

CHAPTER

1

Who Were
These Women?

WHO WERE THESE five exceptional women who became known as the Famous Five? All of them lived in Alberta, although none had been born there. Three of the women came from Ontario, one from Quebec, and one from Britain via India and Ireland. Three were born in 1868, the year after Canada became a country. All five women were married and mothers. Three were provincial politicians. All were devout Christians, accomplished public speakers, feminists, activists, and social reformers.

Despite their impressive individual credentials, some historians have called the group "The Famous One plus Four,"[1] because there is no denying that Emily Murphy was the driving force in the campaign to have women recognized as "persons" under the terms of the British North America (BNA) Act and thereby be granted

4

the right to be appointed to the Senate. But all five of the women contributed to women's, and human, rights in Canada.

Henrietta Louise Muir Edwards

Henrietta Edwards, the oldest member of the Famous Five, was born into a large and prosperous family on December 18, 1849. Her parents were forward-thinking people who were well-connected politically and often sponsored public talks that provided information about progressive issues such as women's rights. They were also devout Christians who had financed the construction of St. Helen's Chapel, the first Baptist church in Montreal.[2]

Before Henrietta's parents married in 1844, they prepared and signed what today would be considered a pre-nuptial agreement, guaranteeing that her mother would be exempt from any financial obligations to her father's businesses and that she would have her own property. In addition, the Muirs' wills divided their estate evenly among their children at a time when it was traditional for daughters to be excluded from inheritances.

Henrietta was a talented artist who studied art in Canada, the United States, and Europe. She specialized in painting miniatures and was so accomplished that she was commissioned to paint a set of dishes as part of the Canadian exhibit at the 1893 World's Fair in Chicago.

She was also active in many of the women's organizations that were forming across the country at the time. She was a feminist and a prohibitionist who strongly believed in the power of women helping women. In 1875, while still living in Montreal, Henrietta and her sister Amelia helped to establish the Working Girls

Henrietta Edwards's legal texts were utilized and admired throughout Canada. GLENBOW ARCHIVES NA 2607-7

Club (later the Working Women's Club), which provided girls and women with rooms, meals, and opportunities to study and learn. The club was a forerunner to the Young Women's Christian Association (YWCA). Together the sisters also formed the Women's Baptist Missionary Society East.

Not surprisingly, given the era, there were no magazines specifically published for working women. Henrietta and Amelia filled that void by opening a company they called the Montreal Women's Printing Office. They employed only women and trained them as typesetters, printers, and compositors. The company published a periodical known variously as *The Working Woman of Canada and Woman's Work in Canada*, which Henrietta illustrated. Remarkably, this endeavour was fully supported by sales of Henrietta's other illustrations and paintings, with her popular likenesses of Sir Wilfrid Laurier and Lord Strathcona consistently earning the most revenue.

As a devout Christian, Henrietta would have been taught that motherhood was a woman's highest calling, so it wasn't surprising that in 1876 she married Dr. Oliver Edwards. Henrietta made a copy of her parents' pre-wedding contract, but the agreement never had to be put in place because, like her parents' marriage, the Edwardses' union flourished. The couple moved to Indian Head and then Fort Qu'Appelle, Northwest Territories (now Saskatchewan), where Henrietta assisted her husband in his medical practice among the local First Nations people. She also created a chapter of the Women's Christian Temperance Union and helped to build a maternity hospital. In 1883, the Edwards family relocated to Fort Macleod (in what is now Alberta), near Lethbridge. By then they had three children, Alice, William Muir, and Margaret.

Having been raised to a life of privilege, Henrietta was shocked at the grinding poverty she saw in Western Canada. She began to investigate the legal system and found that there were no laws to protect women and children who had been abandoned, an all-too-common situation. This would not change unless people became aware of the injustice, so Henrietta set out to educate herself about the law.

When, in 1901, the National Council of Women of Canada (NCWC) published *Women of Canada: Their Life and Work,* it contained one chapter, "The Political Position of Canadian Women," that Henrietta had written. She also assisted with the chapter "Professions and Careers."[3] By 1908 her research led to the publication of her first book, *Legal Status of Canadian Women*, about the situation that had first drawn her attention. It was used as a resource across the country for many years.

Through her legal research, Henrietta came to meet Emily Murphy, who was also looking into the lack of laws protecting women in Alberta, as well as the other women who would gather at Murphy's home for tea in 1927.

National Council of Women of Canada

The National Council of Women of Canada (NCWC) was founded in 1893 by Lady Aberdeen, Ishbel Maria Hamilton-Gordon, Marchioness of Aberdeen. Lady Aberdeen was married to Sir John Campbell Hamilton-Gordon, who was Canada's Governor General from 1893 to 1898.

The NCWC's first meeting was held on October 27, 1893, in Toronto. An astounding fifteen hundred women attended. All were united in their determination to improve the lives of women, families, and communities. Henrietta Edwards, Nellie McClung, Louise McKinney, Emily Murphy, and Irene Parlby were active members of the NCWC, which strongly supported the Persons Case.

In 2018 the organization celebrated 125 years of service in Canada. The National Council of Women of Canada remains an active group today, with chapters in six provinces.

Nellie Letitia Mooney McClung

Nellie McClung was the youngest of the Famous Five and also the best-known member. She was born in 1873 on a farm near Owen Sound, Ontario, but grew up in rural Manitoba. As a child, Nellie

Who Were These Women?

Nellie McClung's contributions changed the course of Canadian women's history. SAANICH ARCHIVES 1981-023-004A.

resented the fact that her activities were more restricted than her brothers' were, and she railed against the inequality. Nellie once shocked her mother by declaring that she would never marry but would remain single and write books for a living. Later the girl softened her stance somewhat and trained as a teacher, a decision that led directly to her marriage—a marriage that did not prevent her from becoming a prolific author.

By the time she was sixteen years old, Nellie Mooney was living away from home and teaching in a one-room schoolhouse near Manitou, Manitoba. These were happy years in the young woman's life. She made friends with many people in her new community, including feminist Annie McClung, who became first her mentor and then her mother-in-law. The two were active members of the Women's Christian Temperance Union and travelled together, speaking out against the evils of alcohol. Nellie quickly became an effective public speaker, and everywhere she went this charismatic woman spoke out in favour of temperance and women's suffrage.

When Annie McClung's oldest son, Wes, came home from university, Nellie was immediately smitten with him. He was working as a clerk in the local pharmacy when Nellie gathered her last three dollars together and went into the drugstore to buy a fountain pen. She later recalled, "I made no pretense of being the Victorian maiden who sits on the shore waiting for a kindly tide to wash something up at her feet." The two young people chatted happily as Wes sold Nellie the pen she wanted. "He had no chance after that!" she said.[4]

Nellie and Wes married in 1896. While Wes operated two pharmacies in Manitou, Nellie began to write the story that became a bestselling novel, *Sowing Seeds in Danny*. In 1910 her second novel was published, also to popular acclaim. All the while, the McClung family was growing. Between 1897 and 1911 they welcomed a daughter and four sons, the last one born just after the family's move to Winnipeg.

Nellie's desire for female equality hadn't changed since childhood, and over these years she also continued her involvement in the fight for the rights of women. When she became aware of the dreadful working conditions endured by immigrant women employed in Winnipeg's factories, Nellie was determined to do something to help. In 1912 she and her friend Edna Nash called on Manitoba's premier, Rodmond Roblin, and insisted that he come with them to see some of those factories. The tour did not last long. Roblin fled from the first building after just a few minutes. The filth, the noise, and the stench of the cold, dark room was too much for him. Nellie and her friend had succeeded in making the most politically powerful person in the province aware of the workers' plight and the immediate need for improved legislation. However, it was clear that in order to effect change, women needed some political clout, and for that they needed the right to vote. (Nellie's role in the suffrage movement is covered in more detail in Chapter Two.)

In 1915 Wes McClung's employer unexpectedly transferred him to Edmonton. The enforced move must have been difficult for Nellie. She had established herself in the Winnipeg community, and she felt there was more she could do for the women of Manitoba. But when she arrived in Edmonton, she soon met Emily Murphy and other feminists and became as active there as she had been in Winnipeg.

Louise Crummy McKinney

Louise McKinney was born into a family of ten children on September 22, 1868, in Frankville, Ontario, a farming community near Ottawa. As a girl she excelled academically and dreamed of becoming a doctor, but given the era and her family's financial constraints, she attended Normal School (teachers' college) instead. She taught at rural schools near Ottawa for several years before moving to North Dakota, where her married sister had settled. Louise accepted a teaching position here, and soon after she met fellow teacher James McKinney. The two were married in 1896 and worked together for the rest of their lives to promote the temperance movement. The couple so admired Frances Willard, founder of the Women's Christian Temperance Union (wctu), that they named their only child, a son, Willard.

In 1903 when the McKinneys moved to Claresholm in what is now Alberta, Louise McKinney brought the wctu with her. She

Louise McKinney travelled the world for her
church and to spread a message of temperance.
CITY OF EDMONTON ARCHIVES EA 10-1579

served in the important post of Resolution Chairman. She set out
the following resolutions for new chapters of the organization:

1. Be it resolved that we acknowledge God as our leader in all
    things, and that we continue to recognize prayer and faith in
    Christ as the foundation principles of our work.

2. That as an organization we urge that men and women every-
    where shall practice and encourage total abstinence from
    alcoholic drinks, and in view of the fact that the liquor traf-
    fic is morally wrong and therefore can never be made legally
    right, we stand for the entire prohibition of its manufacture,
    sale and use.

3. That we put forth the most strenuous efforts for the enforcement of the present law against the sale of cigarettes to minors; and also that we continue our efforts to induce the Dominion government to prohibit the sale, manufacture and importation of the same.

4. That we guard our Lord's day, and that we cooperate with the Lord's Day Alliance in endeavouring to secure better observance of the same. That we do our best to assist trainmen in obtaining Sabbath rest by discouraging Sunday travelling; and that we discourage Saturday night shopping and all other work which tends to prevent a proper observance of the Sabbath Day.

5. That our women be urged to use the limited franchise we have and continue our efforts for the full enfranchisement of our sex, knowing that it is one of our strongest weapons in the battle for the reforms we are seeking.

6. That we earnestly entreat the members of the WCTU to discourage by their example the use of bird plumage for millinery purposes, and that we encourage the formation of humane societies and bands of mercy.[5]

Those were clearly not resolutions for weak-willed women to adhere to, and there is no denying that the goals set out by the resolutions were ambitious and far-reaching—from an outright ban on alcohol to votes for women (as long as their hats were feather-free). There is also no denying the women's dedication to their causes. The WCTU's pledge, spoken at every meeting, was: "I will never falter until this land is freed from the bonds of the distiller, brewer and government company." The groups encouraged members of their communities to sign pledge cards reading: "I hereby promise, by the help of God, to abstain from the use of all intoxicating liquors, including wine, beer, and cider as a beverage." Those cards were decorated with leaves, ribbons, and flowers as well as the phrases "Touch Not," "Taste Not," "Handle Not." There were also slogans such as "Alcohol debauches manhood, debases womanhood, defrauds childhood."

Today it is easy to mock the rigidity of the women's stance— and even at the time, some of the men who felt the full force of the WCTU's efforts retaliated by claiming that those initials really stood for Women Continually Tormenting Us—but the intentions of the temperance movement were admirable. Life was rough for most Canadians in the early twentieth century, and there were few diversions available. Alcohol was a cheap and effective distraction that was rarely used in moderation, and children often suffered from the consequences of the drinking habits of one or both of their parents.

Louise McKinney regularly attended WCTU conferences in the United States and Europe as a speaker, representing WCTU chapters of Canada and especially the Canadian West. These responsibilities no doubt taught her a great deal about manoeuvring within a political setting, skills that held her in good stead for the rest of her life and brought her into contact with Nellie McClung and other temperance activists in Edmonton.

Mary Irene Marryat Parlby

Irene Parlby was the only member of the Famous Five who was not born in Canada. She was born in London, England, on January 9, 1868. Her father was a high-ranking British colonial officer. Irene was the oldest child in the family, and perhaps this is why she enjoyed a particularly close relationship with her father. He encouraged her to attend medical school, but she flatly refused. She maintained that she had already received a well-rounded education in Switzerland and Germany and had found the arts were more to her liking than the sciences.

By the time Irene was eighteen, the family had lived in India and then Ireland before moving back to London in time for Irene's eighteenth birthday. After that celebration, complete with a debutante ball, Irene enjoyed a year-long social whirl before taking another year to travel the world.

In 1896 those travels took Irene on a holiday to visit friends, Alix and Charles Westhead, who had settled in Western Canada. The journey was arduous. After sailing across the Atlantic to Montreal, she took the train to Calgary, where she changed rail lines and continued north to Lacombe. There she was met by a horse-drawn wagon for the final leg of the trip to her friends' rural home. In a short memoir she wrote for the September 25, 1918, edition of *The Grain Growers' Guide*, a weekly newspaper for farmers, Irene recalled,

> My first drive from Lacombe, which was the nearest station, thirty miles away, was a thing of vivid memories—tumbling out of one mud hole into another, doubling up teams to get through, dropping into a creek and praying the bridge of poles was somewhere

under the water and we might be lucky enough to hit the middle of it in the waning light of a summer evening, arriving at the ranch about 11:30 p.m., tired out but thrilled with a feeling of adventure, to find a roaring fire of logs in the living room to welcome us.[6]

Given Irene's privileged, urban upbringing, her positive reaction to the arduous journey might seem astonishing. But clearly, from the moment of her arrival in the Canadian west, Irene was strongly drawn to the wide-open spaces and the possibilities that existed there. "Everything was fresh and the world seemed so young and interesting. Seeing a country in the making is an interest not given to everyone," she remarked.[7]

Not long after she arrived, Irene met Walter Parlby, an Oxford-educated Englishman who, along with his brother, Edward, had settled near the town of Alix (named in honour of Alix Westhead) in what would soon become the province of Alberta. Walter and Irene married in spring the following year, during a blizzard so severe they could not get to the church. Fortunately, Calgary's Bishop Pinkham had already arrived in the area to perform the ceremony, so the venue for the wedding was simply changed to the Westheads' home.

The Parlbys lived in the Alix area for the rest of their lives, although they did go back to England for the birth of their only child, a son, Humphrey, who was born in 1899. Irene's parents, the Marryats, immigrated to Canada in 1905, settled in the Alix area, and lived the rest of their lives here. Many descendants of the Parlbys continue to live in central Alberta and contribute to their communities.

Irene Parlby was a reluctant but effective politician.
GLENBOW ARCHIVES NA 2204-12

Both Irene and Walter were highly regarded and very involved members of the community. Irene always had great concern for the hardships of rural women and children: their isolation and the difficulty accessing education and health care. To this end, she saw to it that a hospital was built, and she helped establish a system of outreach medical and dental care. Irene also started a local public library by soliciting donations of books through newspapers in London, England. Once the library was established, she served as the first president of the library association.

In 1905 the Parlbys travelled to Edmonton for the inauguration of Alberta as a province. This was a meaningful event for Irene, who treasured the memory of being in the company of Governor General Albert Grey and Prime Minster Wilfrid Laurier while they gave speeches from a decorated podium near where ground would soon be broken for construction of the province's legislative building. Walter Parlby played a celebratory game of polo with his teammates for the entertainment of the dignitaries assembled.

Shortly after Walter Parlby and others formed the United Farmers of Alberta (UFA) in 1909, Irene initiated the United Farm Women of Alberta (UFWA), dedicated to improving the lives of women and children in the province. She served as president of that group until 1919. She was, by nature, a shy woman, but overcame that tendency to become an excellent public speaker.

Through her activism she came to know the work of the other women who would make up the Famous Five.

Emily Gowan Ferguson Murphy

Like Irene Parlby and Louise McKinney, Emily Ferguson Murphy was born in 1868. Emily's mother was a prim and proper Victorian lady who tried fruitlessly to subdue her daughter's boisterous behaviour, but her father, a prosperous, well-connected businessman, treated his sons and daughters equally.

From the time she was seven, Emily attended school in a one-room schoolhouse in nearby Cookstown, Ontario. On weekends, she and her siblings were tutored in Latin. They also had weekly handwriting lessons designed to teach them how to write for long periods of time without tiring. Their father wanted to prepare his children to lead successful lives that were of service to others, and he knew this would mean extensive written communication.

Apparently there was still ample time in the Ferguson children's day for getting into mischief. Once, when the siblings drove the family's horse-drawn carriage through town, a neighbour was said to have commented, "There go those young Ferguson devils."[8]

Who Were These Women?

When she was fourteen, Emily left home to attend a private boarding school in Toronto. There, less than two years later, she was introduced to Arthur Murphy, a divinity student. Although he was nearly a dozen years her senior, the two fell in love and immediately became inseparable. Emily took Arthur home to meet her parents, and they apparently approved of their daughter's choice because the wedding date was set for late in the summer of 1887. Emily was nineteen years old.

A few hours before the ceremony, the bride-to-be happily held her wedding dress against her body and pirouetted in front of a large mirror in the hallway of her parents' home. As she did, the mirror suddenly fractured, making enough noise to bring the rest of the family running. Fortunately no one was injured, but there was not enough time to move the broken piece of furniture out of sight before the guests arrived, so Emily's mother hastily covered the cracked mirror with a curtain. The attempted camouflage wasn't entirely successful. All through the wedding ceremony and the reception, Emily felt that people were staring at her apprehensively, wondering if this strange occurrence had been a foreboding omen.[9]

As it turned out, the wedding was the last happy event to be held in the Ferguson family home. A few months later, Emily's beloved father died, and her mother moved away. Shortly after that the house burned to the ground.

Emily and Arthur's marriage thrived, however. The couple remained devoted to one another throughout their lives. They had four daughters, one of whom was born prematurely and only survived for a few months. Through it all, the Murphys' marriage held solid, with husband and wife fully supporting one another in all their endeavours.

Without Emily Murphy the Persons Case might
never have been brought before the Privy Council.
GLENBOW ARCHIVES EA-10-2026

Arthur's career as an Anglican minister meant that the family frequently moved from one small town to another. Emily was young to take on the role of minister's wife, but she took it all in stride and quickly developed leadership qualities. She helped Arthur by investigating topics for his sermons. In doing so, she honed the research skills she would need for the challenges ahead. Everywhere the family went, Emily became involved with the community. She was always genuinely interested in people and made a point to find out about their lives and to help them wherever and in whatever way she could. She began to keep a record of her experiences, which became a reference that served her well in the future.

Who Were These Women?

In the summer of 1898 the church transferred Arthur to England. Emily's mother was aghast at the thought of her daughter uprooting the young family, but Emily, Arthur, and their daughters happily set sail for a great year-and-a-half adventure that changed the course of Emily's life.

England's industrialized economy depended largely on employing cheap labour. Emily was shocked to see the horrendous conditions in the factories where workers, many of them children, toiled in fetid, airless rooms, often for ten hours a day. She began writing down descriptions of the horrors she saw and her reactions to those atrocities. She also made notes about the disparaging way she heard English people speak of Canada and Canadians. Those accounts were the beginning of her career as the social critic and bestselling author "Janey Canuck," a nom de plume that became a lifelong, affectionate nickname for Emily.

By 1901 the Murphys were back on Canadian soil, and Arthur was assigned by the church to do mission work from a base in Toronto. The family settled into a house in a comfortable residential area near the city's High Park. Kathleen and Evelyn, the two older daughters, attended a private school in North Toronto, while little Doris, their youngest surviving daughter and the apple of her mother's eye, stayed at home with Emily.

Later that year, Emily's first book was published. *Impressions of Janey Canuck Abroad* is a series of anecdotes and vignettes loosely based on her experiences while the family lived in London. The book was apparently badly produced but nevertheless sold very well.

A few months later, first Arthur and then Emily contracted typhoid fever. With Arthur unable to work, the family's income dwindled. Emily responded in the only way she knew how; she wrote about their experiences and sold the stories to magazines and newspapers in order to help support the family.

Emily and Arthur had barely recovered from their illnesses when their beloved Doris died of diphtheria in December 1902. She was only ten years old.

Grief engulfed the entire family for months. For a while it seemed as though none of them would ever recover, but in the summer of 1903 the couple decided that Arthur should give up his ministry and the family should move to Western Canada. Emily's alter ego, Janey Canuck, went along for the ride. The family settled in the tiny, isolated community of Swan River, Manitoba, near the Saskatchewan border.

Despite the dramatic difference between the life she had been living in Toronto and life on the Canadian frontier, Emily settled down to enjoy the family's new home in Manitoba. Her first public service project was working to see that a hospital was built in the town. Once it was built, she served as president of the hospital's board.

In her spare time, Emily rode her horse over the prairie and explored the countryside surrounding her new community, always taking careful notes about people, events, and settings she encountered. The country's population was exploding, and people were eager to read everything they could about their new homeland. Janey Canuck had officially arrived in Western Canada, and the timing could not have been better. Emily's second book, *Janey Canuck in the West,* was published in 1907 and quickly became a bestseller.

All the while, Arthur had been hearing talk of the abundant opportunities in Alberta, and he liked what he heard. As Emily explained the situation, "Arthur would like to move to Edmonton. I would like to stay in Swan River. We've agreed to compromise on Edmonton."[10]

When the Murphy family arrived in May 1907, Alberta had only been a province for two years, and Edmonton, the capital city, was a bustling, progressive place. Wealthy matrons in the area were excited to have an author settling in their neighbourhood, so Emily enjoyed a busy social life, but, as she had done wherever the family lived, she once again made a point to explore the surrounding area.

It is ironic that Emily was hesitant to make the move, because Edmonton is where she really came into her own, meeting like-minded women who became her lifelong friends and with whose support she influenced Canadian history.

2

Working Together
(The 1910s)

Temperance and the Right to Vote

All of the Famous Five were actively involved in the temperance movement, and it was work on this cause that led them to become politically active.

The Women's Christian Temperance Union was established in Canada in 1890. Alcohol abuse was a serious problem in many communities, and WCTU activists were convinced that temperance (moderation in the use of alcohol, or abstinence) was necessary to protect women and children. Although there were certainly women who drank, the group's efforts were focused on men, whose drunkenness often resulted in physical and financial harm to their families. Members of the WCTU held women who drank, especially women who were mothers, in even lower regard than alcoholic men.

Working Together (The 1910s)

Initially the activists tried to achieve their ends through education of individuals, but when this was unsuccessful they turned to government to regulate when and where liquor could be sold—or to end sales altogether. Eventually, members of the WCTU came to see that temperance could not be achieved without political power, so winning women's right to vote came to be of prime importance.

On February 9, 1893, WCTU activists in Winnipeg staged a mock parliament in the city's Bijou Theatre. Twenty members of Manitoba's legislature attended the performance, although it is not clear whether Thomas Greenaway, the premier of the province, was among them.[1] The presenters hoped to make the point that "a woman is a rational, independent organism endowed by the Creator with certain natural rights which no one may infringe without wrong-doing."[2] The *Manitoba Free Press* reported optimistically that the politicians who attended—all men, of course—left the theatre "wiser and better" than when they had entered.[3] If so, their newfound knowledge was not reflected in action. A year later, WCTU members were promised that the issue of women's suffrage would be addressed by the Manitoba legislature. But when the scheduled day came, the topic was not even included on the agenda.[4]

Next, the women created a petition and gathered thousands of signatures supporting women's right to vote. Two major figures in the Manitoba chapter of the WCTU, Dr. Amelia Yeomans and journalist Cora Hind, formed the Equal Suffrage Club. Still no progress was made. When Yeomans moved to Calgary in 1904, the suffrage movement in Manitoba lost some of its momentum—though by the mid-1910s, a new generation of activists had picked up the cause and broadened the scope of advocacy.

One of those activists was Nellie McClung, who had already confronted the premier, Rodmond Roblin, about the conditions for immigrant women in factories. On January 28, 1914, she was one of a group of suffragists, inspired by the earlier activists, who rented Winnipeg's palatial Walker Theatre and presented a well-attended play depicting a mock parliament in which women governed. Nellie played the role of Premier Roblin, with other women in the roles of petitioners, and the women's daughters acting as pages. Nellie's sense of comic timing and her skill as a mimic brought down the house as she ruled that men "should always be clad modestly in public."

The reversed gender roles allowed the players to skewer the reasons men gave for not allowing women to have the vote. When a petition was presented to the "premier" requesting that men be allowed to vote, Nellie blustered, in a perfect imitation of Rodmond Roblin's speaking style, "I believe a man is made for something higher and better than voting. Men are made to support families. Politics unsettles men and unsettled men mean unsettled bills, broken furniture, broken vows, and divorce!"[5]

The audience laughed uproariously at the parody, and the women knew they had found an effective way to reflect the travesty of the law as it stood. By the time their performance ended, the amateur actors had changed history. Within two years, Manitoba became the first province to grant the franchise to women, but the privilege was only granted to some women: those who were over the age of twenty-one and of British descent.

Ironically, Nellie McClung was not able to celebrate the victory by voting in the next Manitoba election. In 1915 she and her family moved to Edmonton. Alberta gave women the right to vote in 1916, and soon other provinces were following suit.

When Women Won the Right to Vote

In January 1916 Manitoba became the first province in Canada to grant voting rights to some women in provincial elections, followed a few months later by Alberta and Saskatchewan. Both British Columbia and Ontario granted the same rights in 1917.

In 1918 Nova Scotia was the first Maritime province to allow some women to vote, with New Brunswick following in 1919. Most Prince Edward Island women gained suffrage in 1922, and Newfoundland, which was not a Canadian province until 1949, extended the privilege to women in 1925. It was not until 1940 that Quebec's government granted some women the right to vote.

In 1919 women in the Yukon gained the vote, followed decades later by the Northwest Territories, which then included what is now Nunuvat, in 1951.

Also in 1919, after the end of the First World War, Canadian women became eligible to vote in federal elections, but none of these changes included women or men of Asian descent. This ruling was only rescinded after the Second World War. Indigenous people were finally granted the franchise in 1960.

Now that women could vote, they knew that they would have to become even more politically involved to improve the lot of women and poor families. They had taken up the fight for suffrage in order to advance the cause of temperance; now they turned their attention to prohibition. Prohibitionists, both men and women, reasoned that if the production and distribution of spirits could be stopped, much of the suffering caused by alcoholism would also be stopped.

After leading a successful march in support of prohibition, Nellie McClung, Alice Jamieson, and Emily Murphy celebrated by purchasing new hats and having their photograph taken.
CITY OF EDMONTON ARCHIVES EA-10-2070

In July 1915 hundreds of men and women marched down Edmonton's main street to force a plebiscite on prohibition. The demonstration was such a success that, after it was finished, Emily and Nellie, along with their friend Alice Jamieson, from Calgary decided to celebrate. The trio treated themselves to the purchase of new hats, then went to a photographer's studio where they had their picture taken. No doubt all three women would be pleased to know that photo remains in circulation today.

The prohibitionists' efforts were successful, and in 1915, even before women had the right to vote, Alberta began an eight-year period as a "dry" province.

Alice Jamieson

Although she received little recognition, Alice Jamieson could be considered the sixth member of the Famous Five. She was an active feminist in Calgary, and in 1913 she became the first woman judge in the British Empire. Her original assignment was children's court, but shortly after Emily Murphy became the first female magistrate in the British Empire, Jamieson became her counterpart in Calgary. Like Emily, Alice had to contend with people who questioned her decisions on the grounds that she was not a "person" and therefore not entitled to be a judge.

Emily, Nellie, Louise, Irene, and Henrietta all knew and admired Alice, who was active in women's organizations in Calgary, including the YWCA and the Local Council of Women. Originally from the United States, Alice was a proud Canadian: "I chose to be Canadian," she would say.[6]

Jamieson Place, a high-rise office building in downtown Calgary, commemorates Alice Jamieson and her service.[7] As well, the Calgary Board of Education operates Alice Jamieson School, an all-girls' school for grades four to nine.[8]

The Dower Act

By the end of 1916 many women in Western Canada had the right to vote in provincial elections. The Alberta chapter of the National Council of Women of Canada (NCWC) was determined to make the most of this newfound power by forming a law committee. The committee's mandate was ambitious: to bring security to women and children through the laws concerning marriage, divorce, adoption, property rights, dower rights, protection of children, minimum wage agreements, and widow's allowances.

Henrietta Edwards immersed herself even further in learning everything she could about family law. In 1921 she published a second book, *Legal Status of Women in Alberta*, a companion to her equally well-respected *Legal Status of Canadian Women* (1908). These volumes were widely used as references, a significant recognition of the quality of Henrietta's work, especially considering that she had no formal legal training. Edwards served as the chairperson of NCWC's Legal Committee for thirty-five years, with people and associations across the country relying heavily on her legal expertise. Irene Parlby, who was equally concerned about the welfare of women and children, was vice-chair of the committee.

In the early years of the twentieth century, women had almost no rights under Canadian and Albertan law. For example, a man could sell the farm that he and his wife had worked together to build, and she could be left with nothing. The husband had the right to sell the farm without his wife's agreement and even without consulting her. If the couple had marital problems, he could abandon his wife, leaving her homeless and penniless.

Mothers did not even have legal jurisdiction over their children. A father could put any or all of a couple's children up for adoption without the wife's knowledge or consent. If a husband decided to move away and take the children, he was well within his legal right.

A married woman could not own property. She could hold a job, but her wages from that job belonged to her husband. If a husband died, his wife had no claim to any part of his estate. He could even specify in his will what should happen to their children after his death.[9]

When Emily arrived in Alberta, she had investigated and found that the provincial government was making tentative inroads to protect married women's rights (in 1910, for example, the province passed the Married Women's Relief Act, which provided for women who were left destitute after their husband died), but the changes were grossly inadequate. Something needed to be done. Emily realized that she would have to educate herself about the laws concerning women's and children's rights. She began haunting the legislative library in Edmonton, and although there is no official record of their first meeting, it is possible this is where she connected with Henrietta Edwards.

Emily spoke out about the injustices she saw around her, and the local newspapers apparently thought this eloquent woman with such outrageous ideas made good copy. Before long she had a substantial following of readers.

Concurrently, a wave of feminism was building throughout the world. In 1911, when British suffragist Emmeline Pankhurst visited Edmonton on her North American tour, she met with Emily and other feminists, influencing and reinvigorating the women's activism.

There was much to learn and much work to do in order to accomplish all that needed to be done. Despite the number of years Emily had been away from Ontario, she still enjoyed a close relationship with her brothers, three of whom were lawyers. All of them were extremely proud of the feisty woman their sister had become, and they were always willing to guide her and clarify any legal matters.

Thus armed, Emily and Henrietta worked with Louise McKinney and Irene Parlby to pass the Dower Act, a piece of legislation intended to protect married women by guaranteeing them the right to one third of their husbands' property. They also ensured

passage of the Married Women's Property Act, which gave women
the same legal capacity as men.[10]

Edwards's enduring efforts, she said at the time, were motivated by the people of Alberta, men and women who had worked
to develop the province.

> To no one woman or group of women... is due the splendid legal
> position of women in Alberta. It is due to the Alberta women,
> who, by their courage, endurance and ability did team work with
> their husbands and brothers in all that has made for the devel-
> opment of the Province. The present legal position of Alberta
> women was gained not by militant methods, nor denunciation
> and accusations of men, but by measuring up to the requirements
> of new surroundings and new duties; and also to the generous
> appreciation of Alberta men who have placed the women on
> an absolute equality in all the responsibilities and duties of full
> citizenship.[11]

The four women were all disappointed that, although the
Dower Act was passed in 1917, it did not come into effect until
after the end of the First World War.

Indigenous People

As well as working for the rights of married women, Henrietta
Edwards was concerned about the rights of Indigenous women.
When she arrived in Alberta, she was heavily involved with her
husband's medical practice, which focused on the health of First
Nations people. Her efforts were held in such high regard by the
people of the Blood Reserve in southern Alberta that, in 1903, they

gave her the name "Otter Woman," indicating their great appreciation and respect for her.[12] Henrietta and Oliver Edwards took hundreds of photographs of people and events in the Indigenous communities, which are an invaluable resource today.

In 1917 Henrietta put forward a resolution at an NCWC meeting, declaring that the organization would advocate on behalf of Indigenous women. She kept her word, for the NCWC soon partnered with the Dominion Social Service Council, and Henrietta was appointed to the committee on Indian Affairs. She sought "such legislations as will raise the social status of our Indian women and afford her equal legal protection with our white women."[13] Sadly, in spite of the efforts of Henrietta and her colleagues, that goal has still not been achieved.

Public Policy

Henrietta Edwards also worked with the War Committee on conservation issues during the last years of the First World War and the early post-war years, when both supplies and morale were running low. She was heavily involved in the creation of the federal Department of Public Health as well as the Department of Child Welfare and served as secretary of the National Subcommittee on Thrift and Economy in Canadian Homes.

On May 30, 1920, Edwards spoke in Lethbridge as a representative of the War Committee and urged her audience to understand the seriousness of the post-war crisis. "The world is almost at the point of starvation and it is still the homemaker's duty to reduce waste and needless luxury in food, dress and entertainment. Let's forget about jewelry for the time being. Let's practice economy in the home, use wheat and meat substitutes where possible, make use of leftover foods, minimize waste in cooking and refuse to place bread on our tables until it is twenty-four hours old."[14]

In the spring of 1918 Henrietta, as well as Nellie McClung and Emily Murphy, were invited to a conference in Ottawa, put on by the War Committee. Along with women from other provinces they discussed and recommended health and child welfare policies, as well as food conservation methods, that would help Canada recover from the war.

Members of the Legislative Assembly

While Henrietta Edwards worked with the federal government, Louise McKinney, Irene Parlby, and Nellie McClung served as elected representatives in the Alberta legislative assembly.

The Non-Partisan League, an agrarian Alberta political party (which was eventually absorbed into the United Farmers of Alberta or UFA), recognized Louise McKinney's skills and nominated her to run for office as a member of the legislative assembly. McKinney accepted the nomination because the Non-Partisan League was the only party that did not accept financial support from liquor producers or retailers.[15] In 1917 only a year after Alberta women won the right to vote, McKinney became the first female parliamentarian in the British Empire, winning her Claresholm riding largely on her prohibition platform.

While in office, Louise McKinney worked with Henrietta Edwards and Emily Murphy to draft and pass the Dower Act to protect the financial rights of married women.

Through it all, Louise never gave up her primary calling: a very vocal fight for temperance. She had founded the Claresholm chapter of the WCTU and remained president of that group until 1930.

She was provincial president for twenty-three years and Dominion vice-president from 1908 to 1930. During those years she established an additional forty-three chapters in Alberta.

The Second Female Parliamentarian

Alberta's Military Representation Act, passed in June 1917, created a political constituency of the 38,000 soldiers and 75 nurses serving overseas during the First World War. That group cast ballots in September 1917, electing hospital worker Roberta MacAdams and soldier Robert Pearson to the Alberta legislature. This made MacAdams the second female parliamentarian in the British Empire. She was the first woman to introduce and successfully move a piece of legislation.[16]

By 1921, however, the temperance movement was falling out of favour in North America, and McKinney was defeated by a mere forty-six votes in her bid to serve a second term in the provincial legislature. While she was in office she had served the people, and especially the women, of Alberta effectively. Although the WCTU never again became anywhere near the significant body it once was, Louise McKinney remained loyal to the cause all her life, and in 1928 she represented the Canadian chapters at the World WCTU Conference in Lausanne, Switzerland.

Although McKinney was defeated in the 1921 election, Nellie McClung and Irene Parlby were both elected at that time to represent the Liberal Party and the United Farmers of Alberta, respectively.

Nellie admired William Lyon Mackenzie King, leader of the federal Liberal Party, so much that when she decided to run in

Alberta's provincial election in 1921, she campaigned as a Liberal candidate even though her political views were more in alignment with the United Farmers of Alberta. Nellie won her Edmonton riding, and from then until 1926 she worked closely in the legislature with Irene Parlby, who did represent the UFA.

In 1923 Wes McClung's employer transferred him once again, this time to Calgary. Nellie served the remaining years of her term in office travelling between the legislature in Edmonton and the family's home in Calgary. Despite that onerous commute, Nellie again put her name forward as a candidate when the 1926 provincial election came up, losing by only a few votes. She dealt with her disappointment by spending the next day in her kitchen cooking, baking, and ignoring the telephone every time it rang. The day after that, the wounds of defeat apparently healed, Nellie picked up with her life exactly where she'd left off before her foray into provincial politics.

Irene Parlby, meanwhile, continued to represent Lacombe in the legislature, serving from 1921 to 1935. She was a reluctant candidate, though obviously an effective one, and a diligent parliamentarian. Her road to the legislature began in 1913, when she became the secretary of the Alix County Women's Club. She later reflected, "Little did I think as I accepted the position that I was taking the initial step that was going to plunge me into many years of public life, for which I had no ambition at all."[17]

As mentioned in Chapter One, Parlby joined the Women's Auxiliary of the United Farmers of Alberta before becoming a driving force in the establishment of the United Farm Women of Alberta (UFWA) in 1916. Like the other women's groups in Canada at that time, the UFWA quickly became a significant entity, with sixteen hundred members. Irene was the first president, and she remained heavily involved with the organization for its entire existence. Pioneer Alberta politician and historian Grant MacEwan referred to Parlby as a "distinguished leader."[18]

In 1921 the UFA became a political party with a mandate to defeat the incumbent Liberal Party, which had been in power since Alberta became a province in 1905. Although still claiming not to be interested in politics, Irene agreed to run as a candidate in the upcoming provincial election. She found the campaigning process "nasty,"[19] but in July 1921 the UFA won a majority government, taking 38 of the 61 seats in the legislature. Much to her surprise, Irene Parlby was elected. Premier Herbert Greenfield appointed her to the position of minister without portfolio, and she served in that capacity for fourteen years, earning the affectionate nickname "Minister of Cooperation."

Unlike Emily Murphy or Nellie McClung, who were impatient activists, Parlby accepted the pace at which government worked and once said, "Evolution cannot be brought about by the use of dynamite."[20] She was especially persistent with issues concerning women and children. During the years she served in the provincial government, nearly twenty laws were introduced to protect the welfare of women and children, including the Minimum Wage for Women Act in 1925. She also helped implement improvements to the Dower Act. One piece of legislation that failed was her Community of Property Bill, which would have seen women retain all property they brought into a marriage, as well as all property they received as an inheritance or gift. As well, any property acquired by a couple during the marriage would remain community property. These proposals were seen as too radical.[21]

A few years before she was first elected, Parlby explained her position as a feminist and her view of politics: "Western farm women want no women's party. We value our privilege of working on equal terms with the men of our organization. We have heard much of the horrors of a man-governed world and man-made legislation, but heaven defend us from a world governed solely by women."[22]

Parlby declined to run in the 1935 election, in which the UFA lost all its seats, replaced as government by the new Social Credit Party.

Magistrate Murphy

While Louise McKinney, Nellie McClung, and Irene Parlby served in the legislature, Emily Murphy was making her name in the justice system.

By 1916 groups of forward-thinking women had formed all across the prairie provinces. One of those collectives, the Edmonton Local Council of Women, sent a delegation to observe the proceedings in a local courtroom to make sure that a group of some twenty women, who were being tried for the crime of prostitution, were treated fairly. The judge was appalled by the presence of a delegation of women and told them all to leave, explaining that the trial would include testimony that was not suitable for mixed company and far too graphic for their sensibilities. He was no doubt correct in his assumption that these white, middle-class women had lived their lives protected from the seamy side of life, but his paternalism provoked an unexpected response.

The visitors left the courtroom as they had been ordered to do, but later that day a representative of the Local Council contacted Emily Murphy, who was, by then, well known for her outspoken feminism. Emily agreed with the judge's proclamation that such a case was not fit for mixed company and then, in true Emily Murphy style, she took that judgment one step further by stating that women's cases should be tried in a special court, overseen by a woman.

Emily must have liked her own idea because she approached the province's Attorney General, Charles W. Cross, with the concept. It is impossible to know whether the man genuinely agreed with her suggestion or whether he was merely calling her bluff, but his response was more than supportive. He asked, "When are you ready to be sworn in as police magistrate?" Never one to back down, Murphy accepted the position of judge in a special court just for women and children, and in 1916 she became the first female magistrate in the British Empire. The appointment seems unusual today, given that she had no formal training in law, but that was not a prerequisite in the early days of the twentieth century.

Emily's brothers offered their hearty congratulations. Harcourt, the youngest, sent her a telegram that read: "Let me offer my congratulations to Your Worship. Try to temper your decisions with mercy and do not hand out too much of your own medicine, namely hard labour."

While her oldest brother, Thomas, wrote:

Well done. In fact I say shake, Judge. The fact that none of your brothers have been able to attain to a position on the bench, and as Fate had willed it that someone in the family must be a judge, you simply had to do it to save our face. Again, well done. You beat your brothers to it. While I am at it, Emily, be easy on "them wimmin." That is the one thing I am afraid of—that you may not possess sufficient gallantry to pass over many things.

Her brother William added, "Good morning Judge. Common sense and mercy are necessary attributes; legal knowledge a valuable qualification; pride, and sometimes a bad liver, are curses of most legal administrations."[23]

As was her custom with any task she took on, Emily approached her position as judge with great thoughtfulness and vigour. She began by structuring her courtroom to be a less intimidating place than regular courts. There was no formal witness stand. Instead, the women who were on trial sat in a chair near Magistrate Murphy's desk.

Once when a little girl was called to testify, Emily knew the child was too young to understand the importance of testifying under oath, so she asked if the girl knew about crossing her heart and promising to tell the truth. The youngster nodded before solemnly crossing her heart and giving her evidence. Members of the press who were present were delighted to report that heart-warming human-interest story in their newspapers. Although there is no denying the unique appeal of the anecdote, Murphy's accommodation for the child was not unusual, and often equal parts social work and legal work were done under Magistrate Murphy's auspices.

Not everyone found the woman judge so endearing, however. Because many of the cases she heard involved women burdened with unwanted pregnancies, Emily publicly advocated the use of birth control. In those days, no matter how obviously sensible this suggestion might be, such matters just were not addressed in polite society.

Another problem the new magistrate faced from her first day in court came from one of the most popular and successful lawyers in the city. Eardley Jackson was with the law firm Cormack, MacKie and Van Allen, Barristers. When Judge Murphy ruled against his client on a liquor violation, Jackson declared that he refused to accept any of Emily's decisions because, according to Canada's constitution, the British North America (BNA) Act, she was not a "person."

In his argument, Jackson reasoned that in 1867, when the BNA Act was written, women did not have legal rights to represent themselves. Therefore, when the word "person" was used in the act, that word referred only to males. Being a lawyer, Jackson was able to find a more recent legal precedent for his claim. He referred to a case tried in England in 1876 in which a woman had attempted to cast a vote in an election. She convinced the polling clerk to give her a ballot, but shortly after that she was arrested. When the case came to trial, the court decided that she was guilty and that "women are persons in matters of pains and penalties, but are not persons in matters of rights and privileges." Murphy's appointment to magistrate was clearly a privilege, and therefore a position from which women were specifically excluded.

Murphy's biographer Byrne Hope Sanders quoted the new magistrate as explaining,

The case [was] a breach of the Liquor Act. Before his client pleads, Counsel for the Defence gets to his feet and objects to my jurisdiction as a magistrate. On being requested to state his objection, he argues that I am not a "person" within the meaning of the Statutes. His argument takes up quite ten minutes and in the end is duly noted. Whereupon the hearing of the case proceeds.

On every subsequent case, this man, who is the most popular criminal lawyer in the city, persisted in raising the objection, while I persisted in hearing the whole argument, the thing appealing to my fancy immensely. Other barristers caught up the objection and we had a merry time of it. He was a poor fellow indeed, who could not put up a new aspect of the argument.[24]

Of course, Emily was not going to back down. She exerted the authority that Jackson was questioning by sending him a letter on October 25, 1916, demanding an apology.

I am informed this morning in the Women's Police Court at the conclusion of the case of Rex vs Nora Holt, you, in the presence of several persons made use of the following grossly insulting words—

"To Hell with Women Magistrates, this country is going to the dogs because of them, I would commit suicide before I would pass a sentence like that."

Unless I receive from you an unqualified apology in writing, I shall regretfully be obliged to henceforth refuse you admittance to this Court in the capacity of Counsel.

I have the honour to be, Sir,

Your obedient servant,

Emily Murphy
Police Magistrate for the City of Edmonton[25]

Clearly, Jackson was looking for a fight, and, equally obviously, Emily Murphy was just the woman to give it to him. There is no record of whether the man ever apologized, but he likely did, for it would have been out of character for Emily to let such an omission slide. As it was, the point became irrelevant in 1920 when

Working Together (The 1910s)

Knowing that many of the women and children appearing before her would be frightened, Judge Emily Murphy chose to sit behind a desk rather than a more formal judge's bench.
CITY OF EDMONTON ARCHIVES EA-10-2010

Alberta Supreme Court Justice John Scott pronounced Jackson's argument invalid by declaring that "reason and good sense" made it self-evident that women were, indeed, persons. He added that women were making considerable contributions to the country and therefore had every right to serve in the capacity of magistrate. Despite Scott's ruling in Alberta, though, the fact remained that the BNA Act could be interpreted as excluding women from its purview.

In 1917 Murphy was promoted from city to provincial court, but her career ambitions were far from satisfied. The fact was, Emily had decided that she wanted a seat in the Canadian Senate.

She was certainly qualified for the appointment, having served as the vice-president of the National Council of Women of Canada, the president of the Canadian Women's Press Club, the director of the Canadian Council of Child Welfare, the vice-president of the Canadian Association of Child Protection, the first president of the Women's Canadian Club of Edmonton, the vice-president of the Social Service Council of Canada, and, according to historian Grant MacEwan, "an officer of one grade or another in each of dozens more organizations."[26]

In 1919, as the first president of the Federated Women's Institutes of Canada (FWIC), Emily presided over the FWIC's inaugural conference. One of the resolutions the women decided on during their meetings was that they would press the government to appoint a woman to the Senate.

Two years later, Gertrude E. Budd, a former Albertan who had moved to Quebec and was now the secretary of the Montreal Women's Club, sent a letter to Emily. In it she asked for permission to put Emily's name forward as a candidate for the Senate. Budd reasoned that Murphy would be an ideal candidate considering her accomplishments, especially her experience as a magistrate.

When she filed Budd's letter, Murphy attached a note to it that read, "How it all started. You will see that it didn't emanate from me. They just knew I had fought the 'person' disability in Alberta and had won out."[27]

Little did Emily know in 1919 that the battle to have women appointed to the Senate would take much longer.

3

The Political Battle
(1917 to 1927)

WOMEN'S GROUPS WERE strongly influential in Canada during its first fifty years as a country. Rural women, perhaps as an antidote to their inherent isolation, were especially involved with these organizations. The Women's Christian Temperance Union, the National Council of Women of Canada, and the Women's Institutes were three of the largest and most powerful of those groups.

The first Women's Institute (WI) was formed by feminist Adelaide Hunter Hoodless in 1897 in Stoney Creek, near Hamilton, Ontario. The intent of the organization was to bring women, mostly rural women, together to enrich one another's lives and experiences. The members met once a month, and their meetings typically involved listening to an educational speaker. The WI's focus was on improving the lives of rural women and children, with hygiene and food sciences being a priority. The idea of the WI caught on—independent chapters formed all across Canada, and the concept was exported to the British Isles. (The 2003 movie *Calendar Girls* was loosely based on a project taken on by the Women's Institute chapter in Rylstone, England.)

WI members in Canada recognized that their chapters would have greater political strength if there were a unifying body to oversee and represent the hundreds of local groups and thousands of members. As a result, the Federated Women's Institute of Canada (FWIC) was formed at a meeting in Winnipeg in February 1919 to coordinate the provincial chapters. The fact that Emily Murphy was appointed first president of the national organization indicates the members were in favour of women's equality. And at that inaugural meeting, as described in Chapter Two, the women passed a resolution to press the government to appoint a woman to the Senate.

This resolution was presented to Prime Minister Robert Borden, but after acknowledging receipt, he said that he "was of the opinion that women could not be appointed to the Senate, since they were not persons within the meaning of the [BNA] Act."[1]

The Canadian Senate

The Canadian Senate was created in 1867 under the British North America Act with the aim of giving the regions of Canada representation in parliament. While seats in the House of Commons are assigned based on population (which means the more populous provinces have more representatives), seats in the Senate are assigned by region. As of 2018 there are twenty-four seats for each of four divisions (Maritimes, Quebec,

Ontario, and Western Divisions), plus nine additional seats for Yukon, Northwest Territories, Nunavut, and Newfoundland and Labrador.

Sir John A. Macdonald, Canada's first prime minister, referred to the Senate as a body of "sober second thought," intended to protect the country from an overly partisan House of Commons pushing through reforms that were not in the country's best interests. However, senators are often appointed because they have some kind of connection to the political party in government, so the Senate has tended to be partisan as well. Critics of the Senate cite this as a reason to reform or abolish the institution.

Section 23 of the BNA Act itemized the qualifications necessary to be appointed to the Senate. Appointees must own $4,000 in real estate, as well as having an additional $4,000 in other investments. They must be subjects of the Queen and at least thirty years of age. The qualifications for becoming a Senator remain the same today as they were in 1867.

Section 24 indicated that the "Governor General shall from time to time, in the Queen's name, summon qualified persons to the Senate." Senators are appointed by the Governor General, the Queen's representative in Canada, after consultation with the prime minister.

Initially Senators were appointed for life, but this was changed in 1965 to a mandatory retirement age of seventy-five.

No bill can be passed into Canadian law without the approval of both the House of Commons and the Senate, although the Senate has rarely vetoed legislation. It does frequently carry out extensive investigations into legislation or issues of the day, and has sent legislation back to the House of Commons for amendment before it is passed in the Senate.

When Alberta senator Peter Talbot died in December 1919, Canadian women's organizations were hopeful that this vacancy would be a chance for a woman to become a senator. Much to their disappointment, Prime Minister Robert Borden still did not see the opening as an opportunity for a change. He referred to the BNA Act's wording, which he maintained had to be followed exactly as it had been written.[2] The act used masculine pronouns to identify an individual and the word "persons" to describe more than one individual, implying that "persons" were, by definition, male.

Despite this ruling, organizations and individuals continued to petition the government to appoint a female senator. By 1921 the woman they were specifically suggesting for the position was Emily Murphy.[3] As mentioned in Chapter Two, Gertrude Budd, secretary of the Montreal Women's Club, requested Murphy's permission to put her name forward. The group's publicity convener sent the nomination to Charles Doherty, Minister of Justice. In due course, the Justice Minister replied, unequivocally, that women were not qualified to serve in the Senate because, according to the BNA Act, women were not persons.

When Murphy learned of the decision, she summed up her feelings succinctly in a note she wrote to Nellie McClung, indicating that she considered the response to be just "the same old rigamarole."[4]

A Change of Leader

Robert Borden retired from politics in July 1920, and Arthur Meighen became leader of the Conservative Party and Canada's prime minister, but his reaction to the idea of a female senator was only minimally better than Borden's. Ever the politician, Meighen stated that he too would like to see a woman in the Senate, but in order for that to happen he was sure the BNA Act would have to be amended, and that, he warned, would be a lengthy process. There is no record of Meighen making any attempt to instigate the amendment process during his eighteen-month term, so no changes were made.

He did ask for an opinion from government lawyer Edmund Newcombe, who responded, "In the absence of any precise authority to the contrary I hold that they are not qualified. There is no Latin word to describe a Senatress."[5]

This unbending stance did not stop women's groups across the country from continuing to put Murphy's name forward for appointment. Copies of petitions were even left in stores and businesses across the country for citizens to sign before they were sent to Ottawa. According to Murphy's first biographer, Byrne Hope Sanders, "Hundreds of prominent persons of both sexes, including the Mayor and all the Aldermen of Edmonton, and organizations representing a membership of over 2,000,000 persons, asked for her appointment." Nellie McClung took to Canada's newspapers to promote her friend's cause, as did many others.[6]

The Public's View

Many of the country's newspapers and magazines supported the women's campaign and wrote editorials confirming their positions. The fact that all those requests were consistently denied did not deter Emily Murphy. Ever the optimist, she was instead heartened by the support of so many different organizations.

All this energy was somewhat offset by the growing number of Canadians who thought the Senate was an outdated and ineffective institution that should be scrapped entirely. People who subscribed to this view felt that Murphy was wasting her time, so the support that the women's efforts might have had was somewhat compromised. Grattan O'Leary, a journalist with *Maclean's* magazine, wrote this unflattering description of the Senate chambers in January 1928:

> In the crimson-cushioned halls of that cathedral-like chamber, the air is warm and heavy. It drags upon you until you wilt and your head swims, and the faces of its members grow hazy. In that indolent atmosphere, so remote from the vital world outside, there is an invitation to relax and grow bored and cease to care. Aged men sit heavily in their seats, mumble wearily through their business, compressed and dull and discouraged.

In 1921 Nellie McClung, on behalf of the NCWC, approached Charles Doherty with another request, for either a change to or a reinterpretation of the BNA Act.[7] Doherty passed the correspondence along to Deputy Minister W. Stuart Edwards, who, by coincidence, was a nephew of Henrietta Muir Edwards's husband. Edwards was sympathetic to the women's cause and did not interpret the BNA Act as excluding women from the Senate. However, the reaction from the government did not change.

As Emily Murphy's name was frequently mentioned as a candidate for the Senate, she realized that she needed to be careful not to appear to be campaigning for herself. In a 1920 letter to the editor of *Women's Century*, a Canadian publication, Emily wrote that she was sure a suitable candidate could be found in Eastern Canada.[8] She did not want her fight to have women become senators seem selfishly motivated by her own ambitions, so she took a step back and let other people, the nation's feminists, speak on her behalf.

A few months later, Gertrude Budd approached Meighen again and stressed to him that women's groups all across the country— the Women's Christian Temperance Union, the Imperial Order Daughters of the Empire, the Canadian Women's Press Club, and every chapter of the Women's Institutes—shared her opinion. Then she obliquely reminded Meighen that there would be an election in the near future, and now that women had the vote, their opinion could make or break any candidate's campaign.

Nellie McClung was heavily involved with many women's groups, and she was also internationally recognized and admired. She had spearheaded the movement that won Manitoba women the right to vote, and she had played a significant role in the victory for Alberta women. She was an effective speaker, an author, and a reformer. In a word, McClung was powerful, and with these credentials she also approached Prime Minister Meighen, suggesting that nominating Emily Murphy for a position in the Senate would be a wise thing to do.

Other members of the Women's Institutes forwarded copies of the ruling by Alberta Supreme Court Justice Scott that stated women were fit to be appointed to the position of magistrate. They also made reference to the Interpretation Act, which Emily's brother had noted specified that references to the male gender were intended to include females also. But no one's efforts resulted in any change.

Clearly the women of Canada were not going to let such an inequitable matter rest, and the government began receiving an onslaught of petitions signed by thousands of people, both men

and women, from across the country. Some of these appeals specified that Emily Murphy should be appointed to the Senate, while
others were more general, simply demanding that women be
acknowledged as qualified for nomination.

A Minority Government

When William Lyon Mackenzie King defeated Meighen in the
December 1921 federal election, he promptly promised that he
would ensure the necessary changes were made to the BNA Act
to allow women to be nominated to the Senate. But King's victory
was so slim that he had the dubious honour of leading the country's first minority government. He had won very little support in
the West and carefully meted out Senate seats to influential men in
the western provinces who could help his popularity. Appointing a
woman, especially one as argumentative as Emily Murphy, might
alter his tenuous balance of authority.

Nellie McClung, however, had great confidence in Mackenzie
King, just as she did in her ambitious friend Emily Murphy. In
January 1922 she sent the new prime minister a letter of congratulations and added, "I also wish to respectfully draw your attention
to the fact that there are no women in the Upper House [the Senate
is also referred to as the Upper House or the Red Chamber] and
that I think it is about time there were."[9] Then she specified that
Emily Murphy would make an excellent choice for that post. King
did not respond to the letter.

Although women seemed no closer to the Senate, in February
1923 a new name was floated for consideration if the Red Chamber
ever was opened to them. Calgary's Council of Women proposed
that Henrietta Edwards be nominated as the first woman senator.

The group said that the appointment of Edwards would be in recognition of her "intensive study of law and the many reforms brought about through the work of the laws committee, of which she is the national convener."

A few months later, in June 1923, Alberta senator Amédée-Emmanual Forget died. Murphy's supporters swung into action again with a petition that read:

Whereas the women of Canada are without representation in the Senate of Canada,

And whereas, measures affecting the welfare of women and children, together with private statues relating to divorce are considered by the said Senate, without the advice and assistance of any representative of women,

And whereas there is at present a vacancy in the Senate in Alberta which requires to be filled,

And whereas Mrs. Emily Murphy is well qualified to fill such a position of trust by virtue of her training and experience acquired as a police magistrate and judge of the Juvenile Court in and for the province of Alberta, and to represent the women of Canada by virtue of her connection with various women's societies... your petitioners pray that the said Mrs. Murphy will be appointed to the said Senate, in order that the said Senate might be better qualified to consider matters concerning the interest of women and children of Canada.[10]

That petition did no more good than any of the previous ones. The excuse this time was that Forget had been a Roman Catholic, so another member of that religion should take his place.

Despite the pledge he had made when he was elected, King said no more about bringing women to the Senate until 1924, when he spoke to the Women's Canadian Club of Calgary. At that event he declared once again that he would make sure this important issue was addressed, and that the slight to women was corrected.[11] He was certainly not the first or last politician to fail to keep his promise.

In November 1925 Alberta senator Sir James Lougheed died. Nellie McClung lost no time in writing to Prime Minister King, expressing her regret at the great statesman's passing and bluntly adding, "Rumours are floating about as to who shall be his successor. It would be a wonderful triumph for the belief that we have held in Liberal fairness to women if Mrs. Murphy should be appointed. Forty thousand women have, through their societies, asked for her. Don't ignore them."[12]

Instead, in June 1926, King appointed Daniel Edward Riley, of High River, Alberta, to the Senate.[13] In the meantime, Nellie McClung had been using her many speaking engagements to keep the topic of women in the Senate in the forefront of Canadian women's minds, with a suggestion that her friend Emily would be an excellent candidate. In 1926 McClung addressed an audience shortly after the Senate rejected legislation for an old-age pension. She declared, "It is high time to get new blood into the moribund body... The old men lack imagination... If we have a woman there, like our Mrs. Murphy, I doubt if the care of our old people would have been so summarily dismissed."

Nellie closed those remarks with a statement reflecting her innate philosophy that groups of women can accomplish a very great deal: "We can have women [in the Senate] if we stand together."[14]

However, although the women's efforts, with the backing of thousands of Canadians, had now covered the terms of three prime ministers, they were only slightly closer to being appointed to the Senate than they had been in 1917. Emily Murphy had lost much of her faith in the ability of the political process to resolve the BNA Act's ambiguity regarding women. She knew that she had to try another tack.

In 1927 Emily was discussing the matter with her brother William, Mr. Justice Ferguson, who had become a highly respected and extremely knowledgeable judge, for an opinion and advice. He turned to the Interpretation Act of 1850 (also known as Lord Brougham's Act) and determined that words specifying references to the "masculine gender shall include females." This would seem to have been definitive, indicating there was nothing in the law to prevent Emily Murphy from being appointed to the Senate, but, again, the government conceded nothing.[15]

And so the legal battle began.

CHAPTER

4

The Legal Battle
(1927 to 1929)

ON AUGUST 5, 1927, Emily Murphy wrote the following letter to her friends Henrietta Muir Edwards, Nellie McClung, Louise McKinney, and Irene Parlby.

Enclosed you will find a copy of Section 60 of the Supreme Court Act of Canada... with also a letter to the Governor General in Council, which letter I am asking you to be good enough to sign and return to me by registered mail as soon as possible.

You will recall that the National Council of Women, the Women's Institutes, the Women's Church [*sic*] Temperance Union, University clubs and other of our organizations, in convention, submitted resolutions to the Honorable Prime Minister at Ottawa, requesting of him that women be admitted to the Senate of Canada, thus permitting us to secure our full enfranchisement.

As a result, with the approval of the Federal Cabinet, on June 25, 1923, in the printed "Orders of the Day," a motion was submitted by the Hon. Senator McCoig of Chatham, Ontario, asking the members of the Upper Chamber that an address might be presented to His Most Excellent Majesty, the King, praying that he might be graciously pleased to give his consent to the submission of a measure to the Parliament of the United Kingdom to amend the British North America Act, 1867, so that "a female person shall be deemed qualified to be summoned to the Senate if she has reached the full age of thirty years and is either a natural born subject of the King, or a subject of the King naturalized under the provisions of any Act of the Parliament of Great Britain, or of any British Dominion or possession of the Parliament of Canada.

When this was read in the Canadian Senate, the Honorable Senator McCoig failed to speak to the motion; neither did he appear to speak upon the same at any subsequent day when it was called so that the motion was never discussed. Since then, this motion has not been placed before the House.

As four years have elapsed, and as it is now held by a large and important body of opinion that such proposed amendment was not, and is not necessary, it has therefore become highly desirable that this matter be determined without further delay in order that the women of this Dominion—comprising approximately one half of the electorate—may enjoy their full political rights on the same terms as these are, or may be, enjoyed by men.

It may here be pointed out that while in 1923, women generally were gratified in having Senator McCoig's motion placed before the Senate of Canada, with a possible prospect of its being later submitted to the House of Commons for added appeal to His Majesty, we have now come to realize that the matter is one which cannot with any degree of fairness be submitted for decision to a body of male persons, many of whom have expressed themselves towards it in a manner that is distinctly hostile. Undoubtedly, our proper procedure under these circumstances is to take advantage of a friendly recourse to the Supreme Court of Canada as provided for in Section 60 of the Supreme Court Act.

You will see by the copy of the Supreme Court Act which I enclose that "interested persons" may refer matters of law or fact touching the interpretation of the British North America Acts, 1867 to 1886,... to the Governor-General in Council requesting that the matter at issue be referred to the Supreme Court of Canada for its hearing and consideration...

As the matter referred to in our letter to the Governor General is purely a technical one, I have not thought it necessary to submit the matter to Canadian women generally, they having already endorsed the principle, but only to the few "interested persons" as specifically required by the Act, these being all from the Province of Alberta and women reasonably capable of giving an account of the principles that actuate them should they be required to do so...

I do not feel it even remotely necessary to urge upon you the extreme desirability of your lending your much-valued influence to this matter, which is so closely allied with the political, social and philanthropic interests of all Canadian women.

Yours very sincerely,
Emily F. Murphy

The missive was certainly a better example of a business letter than a personal one, but even though the recipients were her friends, the topic was all business to Emily, and the letter clearly demonstrated Murphy's knowledge and deep concern for the matter. Once she had received positive replies from all four women, she began to draft the most important letter she would ever write.

This is the letter, addressed to the Governor General, that she and the other four women signed on August 27, 1927.

Sir:

As persons interested in the admission of women to the Senate of Canada, we do hereby refer to the Supreme Court of Canada for hearing, consideration and adjudication the following constitutional questions:

I. Is the power vested in the Governor-General in Council of Canada, or the Parliament of Canada, or either of them, to appoint a female to the Senate of Canada.

II. Is it constitutionally possible for the Parliament of Canada under the provisions of the British North America Act, or otherwise, to make provision for the appointment of a female to the Senate of Canada?

These questions are respectfully referred for your consideration pursuant to Section 60 of the Supreme Court Act, R.S.C. 1906, Cap. 139.

We have the honour to be, Sir,
Your obedient servants,
(sgd.) Henrietta Muir Edwards (Macleod)
Nellie L. McClung (Calgary)
Louise C. McKinney (Claresholm)
Emily F. Murphy (Edmonton)
Irene Parlby (Alix)

The document, with the five women's names and signatures in alphabetical order, was sent to Ottawa, where it was forwarded to the Department of Justice.

In the letter, Emily was asking if it was within the Canadian government's constitutional power to appoint a woman to the Senate or to amend the BNA Act in order to appoint women to the Senate. She specifically did not ask if women were persons according to the act, in part because there had already been several opinions expressed by ministers, lawyers, and others from both Conservative and Liberal governments, stating that women were not persons.

Emily was well aware that she might not receive a favourable ruling from the Supreme Court, but for valid reasons she did not want to proceed alone. She did not want to be seen as eager for a Senate post herself, but she also wanted the support and credibility that Edwards, McClung, McKinney, and Parlby would bring to the inevitable next leg of her campaign.

The Legal Battle (1927 to 1929)

In a paragraph of her December 1932 letter to Mrs. J.P. Hynes, Murphy recalled that it was her "intention to request that these four splendid women—'interested' but not 'persons'—make with me an inclusive tour of Canada urging the electors thereof to demand a revision of the *British North America Act*. For this reason I selected appellants who were outstanding representatives of the different political parties. Two of these had been Members of the Alberta Legislature and one was a Cabinet Minister."[1]

It is clear that Emily Murphy was fully aware of the reasons she chose the four other women to be her co-appellants. At the time, however, she only took Nellie McClung into her confidence with details of the strategy.

National News

"The Persons Case," as it was popularly known, had become national news, and many newspapers, magazines, and organizations in the country offered support to the women's campaign. The *Canadian Morning Chronicle*, the daily newspaper in Halifax, Nova Scotia, proclaimed that "Mrs. Murphy has in almost every sphere of activity she ever entered, become of nation-wide repute. Although she is very much of the West, she is first and last, of Canada."

The *Toronto Star* noted, "The Senate does not know what it missed. Perhaps it never will, but everybody who knows the Judge knows it has missed a treat. In the Senate where humour is so dry as to have been withered before it gets by the Black Rod, they would much enjoy the lady from Edmonton, but not half so much as the lady would enjoy the Senate."

And the *Fort William Times Journal* commented, "with Mrs. Murphy in the Senate, the good comradeship of Canada will be well represented in the Upper House."[2]

Meanwhile, in Ottawa, Ernest Lapointe, the Minister of Justice, acknowledged that the concerns addressed in the letter signed on Emily Murphy's front porch the previous August had sufficient national implication that the argument could be taken to the Supreme Court of Canada. Furthermore, because the case was deemed to be "an act of justice to the women of Canada," the government would cover the legal fees.[3]

Before he sent the petition to the Supreme Court, however, Lapointe changed the wording by adding the question that Murphy had purposely avoided: "Does the word 'persons' in Section 24 of the British North America Act, 1867, include female persons."[4]

Lapointe then sent a copy of his amendments to Murphy, who was understandably outraged at not being consulted before the changes were made. On November 9, 1927, Emily wrote to the Deputy Minister of Justice, W. Stuart Edwards, to say that Lapointe's changes fundamentally altered the essence of the original petition. Her annoyance is obvious right from the first sentence of her letter to Edwards.

> We respectfully beg to point out that the question referred to the Supreme Court by the enclosed Order-in-Council is not the one submitted by your petitioners either in word or in meaning and is, in consequence, a matter of amazement and perturbation to us.

One wonders if the Minister of Justice had ever before been told that a decision he had made was met with "amazement and perturbation."

Murphy then reiterates that her original letter had specifically asked if the cabinet (that is "the Governor-General in Council") or Parliament could appoint women to the Senate, whereas Lapointe's revised document asked whether the word "persons" in the BNA Act included females. She speculates, rather pointedly, that Lapointe's apparent confusion may have arisen from previous discussions when government officials determined that, under the BNA Act, "male persons only may be summoned to the Senate." She insists that the re-worded question be withdrawn. She also notes that the women's second question—whether, constitutionally, Parliament could appoint a woman to the Senate—was omitted from Lapointe's version of the document altogether.

Perhaps fearing that the two questions she asked in her August 27 letter were in some way inadequate or unclear, Emily added a third question, perhaps to clarify her second question about the constitution. "If any statute be necessary to qualify a female to sit in the Senate of Canada, must this statute be enacted by the Imperial Parliament [that is, the British Parliament, in London, England], or does power lie with the Parliament of Canada or the Senate of Canada?"

Murphy closed her letter in a milder tone by writing, "We can have no doubt concerning the kind intent and good will of the Honourable Minister of Justice and that he, accordingly, will take the necessary procedure to refer these important and well concerned questions on the Supreme Court of Canada in their original wording and in their given order."[5]

The Petition to the Supreme Court of Canada

November 1927

In the matter of a reference as to admission of women to the Senate of Canada

The humble petition of Mrs. Henrietta Muir Edwards, Mrs. Nellie L. McClung, Mrs. Emily F. Murphy, Mrs. Louise C McKinney and the Honorable Irene Parlby, sheweth as follows:

1. That your petitioners are respectfully referring to this Honorable Court, through His Excellency the Governor General, for hearing and consideration, pursuant to Section 60 of the Supreme Court Act, the three following questions upon constitution:

    (a) Is power vested in the Governor General of Canada, or the Parliament of Canada, or either of them, to appoint a female to the Senate of Canada?

    (b) Is it constitutionally possible for the Parliament of Canada, under the provisions of the British North America Act, or otherwise, to make provisions for the appointment of a female to the Senate of Canada?

    (c) If any statute be necessary to qualify a female to sit in the Senate of Canada, must this statute be enacted by the Imperial Parliament, or does power lie with the Parliament of Canada or the Senate of Canada?

2. That the questions so referred are questions of general public importance and your petitioners, as representative of a class of persons interested and affected by these questions are desireous [*sic*] of being represented by Counsel upon the hearing of argument of the questions so referred.

3. That your petitioners having regard to the special nature of the questions so referred, consider that they ought not, as individuals, to be required to bear the expense of retaining counsel to prepare and present the argument on their behalf upon the said question.

Your Petitioners therefore humbly pray that this Honourable Court will be graciously pleased, in its discretion, in pursuance of the provisions of section 60, sub-section 5, of the Supreme Court Act, to request the Honourable Newton W. Rowell to appear on their behalf on the hearing of argument of this reference and to argue the case as to their interests therein; the reasonable expenses thereby occasioned to be paid by the minister of Finance as the statue in that behalf provided.

And your petitioners will ever pray etc., etc.,

Signed
Henrietta Muir Edwards
Nellie L. McClung
Emily F. Murphy
Louise C. McKinney
Irene Parlby

Wanted: The Best Lawyer Possible

Emily Murphy knew that she would need a uniquely qualified lawyer to shepherd her petition through the legal system. Interestingly, she didn't choose one of her lawyer brothers. Instead she asked the Honourable Newton Wesley Rowell, a well-respected Ontario lawyer, to take it on. The federal government had determined that this case was of sufficient importance to Canadians that the costs would be fully covered, so Murphy knew she could afford the best.

Rowell had been born on a farm near London, Ontario, in 1867. As a young man he could not afford to attend law school, so he took a junior position with a local law firm instead in order to learn on the job. Rowell must have been a diligent and extremely clever trainee because in 1891, when he wrote the bar exams, his marks were the second highest in the Law Society of Upper Canada. By 1902 he was awarded the designation King's Counsel (KC), indicating that his law practice was important, exemplary, and contributed positively to the legal profession.

Like the five women who were fighting the Persons Case, Rowell was intelligent, determined, and very used to succeeding. Both he and his wife had strongly supported temperance and women's suffrage. He was politically astute and had served as leader of the Liberal opposition in the Ontario legislature from 1911 to 1917. In 1917 he was elected to the federal Parliament and became the first federal Minister of Health in 1919. He played a significant role in establishing the League of Nations, forerunner to the United Nations. He was also vice-chair of Canada's War Committee, and in 1918 he asked Emily Murphy, Nellie McClung, and Henrietta Edwards to attend a conference held by the War Committee in Ottawa. In his invitation he explained that women from all parts of Canada would be meeting to discuss women's increased involvement with the war effort. This is certainly an indication that Rowell thought as highly of the women who were to make up the Famous Five as they did of him.

The case was heard in Ottawa on March 14, 1928, Emily Murphy's sixtieth birthday. Representatives from each provincial government were invited to attend, but only one from Quebec (against the change) and one from Alberta (in favour) were present. Chief Justice Frank Anglin, as well as Justices Duff, Lamont, Mignault, and Smith, listened intently as Wesley Rowell argued the women's case. Opposing Rowell were Lucien Cannon, the Solicitor General, and Eugene Lafleur and Charles Plaxton from the federal Attorney General's office, as well as Charles Lanctot of the Attorney General of Quebec's office.

Both sides went into the courtroom well prepared. Rowell's written argument was concise, only three pages in length, but was supported by a thirty-three-page appendix citing the laws and precedents on which he had based his case. The opposition's argument filled twenty-four pages, with a nine-page factum and a sixty-five-page appendix. The province of Quebec also opposed the women's case and presented an eleven-page factum.

The Supreme Court Decision

A month and ten days later, on April 28, the Supreme Court announced its decision. Chief Justice Frank Anglin declared,

> There can be no doubt that the word "persons" when standing alone... includes women. It connotes human beings—the criminal and the insane equally with the good and the wise citizen, the

minor as well as the adult. Hence the propriety of the restriction placed on its use in this section which speaks of "fit and qualified" persons. The terms in which the qualifications of members of the Senate are specified in Section 23 import that only men are eligible for appointment. [Therefore] women are not eligible for appointment by the Governor General to the Senate of Canada under Section 24 of the British North America Act, 1867 because they are not "qualified persons" within the meaning of that section. The question submitted, understood as above indicated, will, accordingly be answered in the negative.[6]

And so, astonishingly, that august body had determined that women were not persons. In defense of their decision, the judges reasoned that the BNA Act had to be interpreted in the context of its time. In 1867 women did not have the privilege of holding any public office, so the Act could not have been referring to women in the use of the word "persons."

Decades later, feminist historian and author Catherine Cleverdon outlined the Crown's position in five concisely worded statements.

Any interpretation of the BNA Act must have regard for the period when the act was passed and new ideas should not be allowed to colour the interpretation; no women were holding offices in 1867. The Act showed that it did not have any intention of including women by its use of masculine pronouns throughout... Women in 1867 were under every conceivable form of legal incapacity and barred from public functions so how could it be supposed that the drafters of the Act meant to include them? That women were not permitted in the House of Lords so would it be reasonable to assume they were intended to sit in the Canadian upper house?[7]

Murphy learned of the decision in a telegram Rowell sent from Ottawa. The terse communication read: "Regret Supreme Court have answered question submitted to them in the negative."

Publicly Murphy kept her composure, only saying that she was sure the Supreme Court had ruled "in all sincerity."

Mary Ellen Smith, a member of the British Columbia legislature, responded much more dramatically: "The iron dropped into the souls of women in Canada when we heard that it took a man to decree that his mother was not a person."[8]

Even the Minister of Justice, Ernest Lapointe, was shocked by the decision. He assured Emily and her associates that he would look into the possibility of having the BNA Act revised. This was not enough for Emily Murphy, Henrietta Edwards, Nellie McClung, Louise McKinney, and Irene Parlby. They agreed that they would take their case to the Privy Council in England, then Canada's highest court of appeal.

5

The Judicial Committee of the Privy Council (1928 to 1929)

ON MAY 2, 1928, Emily Murphy wrote to her co-appellants, forwarding to them the appeal she had sent to the Governor General in Council, which asked that their case "in regard to the meaning of 'Persons'... be referred on appeal to the Judicial Committee of the Privy Council."[1]

Murphy was careful not to criticize politicians or justices, saying, "While we regret that the decision of the Supreme Court of Canada was not favourable to our cause, I am sure we are agreed that their decision was a sincere one and should not be adversely criticized by any of us."

She went on to state that their appeal should not be seen "as in anywise expressing a lack of confidence in the determination of the ... Minister of Justice, and his colleagues of the Cabinet to devise means whereby the B.N.A. Act may be amended to permit of women sitting in the Senate of Canada." But she said that the move to amend the act could be blocked by a political change in Ottawa or by the dissent of one or more provinces. A positive ruling by the Judicial Committee of the Privy Council would prevent any such objections.

In the letter to her friends and colleagues, Emily noted the positive impact of the Supreme Court case among Canadian women, who, "for the several years past, ... owing to what appeared to be a hopeless situation, took comparatively little interest in this matter of the interpretation of the word 'Persons' in Section 24 of the B.N.A. Act." She believed their appeal to the Supreme Court of Canada for a ruling "gave to the women of all parties a renewed hope and had the effect of stimulating them to something approaching definite action. We have every reason to felicitate ourselves in this behalf."

And even if they were unsuccessful at the Privy Council, Emily was optimistic: "Of the ultimate results, I have not the slightest doubt. Nothing can prevent our winning. Every editor in Canada except those in Quebec is backing us in the appeal. When the time is ripe, it can reasonably be predicted that the French Editors will also concede in the justice and propriety of our claim."

She concluded the letter by noting a precedent that went as far back in history as one could legitimately reach.

It is also truly encouraging—and we may take the assurance to our hearts—that no extension of the franchise has ever been defeated since John, the King of England, signed the Magna Carta at Runnymede.

In July 1928 Emily wrote to W. Stuart Edwards, the Deputy Minister of Justice, who had been supportive of the women's cause, commenting again on her optimism regarding the referral to the Judicial Committee of the Privy Council. She said that she had been closely studying several Supreme Court of Canada judgments, and it was "apparent that their conclusions have been based upon things extraneous, or upon matters or circumstances not found within the British North America Act itself."[2] This revived her hope that her brother's reading of the Interpretation Act might prevail: "We contend that by virtue of the Imperial Interpretation Act passed prior to the British North America Act the word 'person' must be construed as including both sexes, no contrary intent being shown."

But now all she could do was wait for the case to be heard and the judges to rule. And sadly, as she waited, her brother William, who had been so helpful and supportive of her, died on November 9, 1928.

The Judicial Committee of the Privy Council

Appearing before the Judicial Committee of the Privy Council (JCPC) was a great honour as well as a great responsibility for members of the legal community. Luckily, Newton Rowell had experience arguing cases before the JCPC. This was no doubt a comfort to the five women in Alberta, all of whom knew this case would not be settled easily. In addition, Rowell was acknowledged as a Canadian constitutional expert. In short, it would have been difficult to find a lawyer more suitable to guide the "Persons Case" through the legal labyrinth to a successful conclusion.

With his adult daughter, Mary, along for the adventure, Rowell left for England in June 1929. Father and daughter set up housekeeping in a furnished flat near the heart of London. And then they waited.

Back at home, Emily Murphy grew frustrated with the delays. Rowell wrote to tell her that every case on the JCPC's agenda was taking longer to see through to completion than had been initially estimated. In the meantime, he kept himself busy with social and political obligations. By the middle of July the novelty of being abroad must have worn off for Mary because she sailed back to Canada and left her father to concentrate on the most important case of his career as a lawyer.

Ironically, the delays that so aggravated everyone involved with the Persons Case might actually have worked in their favour, because John Sankey, the judge who eventually presided over the case, was a forward-thinking man who took over the position of Lord Chancellor of the Privy Council only a few weeks before the case finally came to the top of the JCPC's agenda. Sankey's predecessor had been a man with a much more conservative outlook on life, so if the case had been heard earlier, the decision might have been disappointingly different. The delay also meant, though, that Sankey did not have much time to familiarize himself with the details of the case.

While Sankey was the lead magistrate, he was flanked by four other judges, and their opinions mattered as well. Charles John Darling was a progressive man and likely to be in favour of viewing women as persons. Henry Edward Duke (Lord Merrivale) specialized in matrimonial law. Thomas Tomlin was widely admired for his common sense, and it's reasonable to assume that he too would be looking toward a favourable ruling. Lancelot Sanderson had served as Chief Justice of the High Court of Judicature of Calcutta for many years, which might have influenced his opinions about "the colonies" one way or another.

The Appeal Is Heard

The JCPC began hearing the appeal on July 22, 1929, and the lawyers' presentations took four days. Emily Murphy could have been in the courtroom but, as always, she had decided to put the interests of the case before her own interests. Murphy had written to Henrietta Edwards, Nellie McClung, Louise McKinney, and Irene Parlby to explain that she "had thought of attending... indeed had intended to, but upon mature consideration thought it would only prejudice our cause."[3] British feminists were far more strident than their Canadian counterparts, and Murphy did not want to be associated with their more militant approach for fear that it would jeopardize all the years of work that had brought them to this court of last appeal. As a result, not one Canadian woman sat in the courtroom where an important facet of their future would be decided.

Alberta's Attorney General, John F. Lymburn, was in the courtroom to follow the progress of the hearing. He later confirmed to Emily Murphy that she had made a wise choice when she selected Newton Rowell to present the case before the Privy Council. He assured Murphy that Rowell "presented a wonderful case... marshaled in a masterly and logical way."[4]

Lukin Johnston, a reporter from the Canadian Press, was also in the courtroom. He noted that, "in a quiet room at Number One, Downing Street, five great judges, with the Lord Chancellor of England at their head, and a battery of bewigged lawyers from Canada and from England, are wrestling with a question, propounded on behalf of their sex, by five Alberta women."

The scribe went on to describe the courtroom, with its high ceilings and book-lined walls, where Lord Sankey sat at a semi-circular table, flanked by the four other judges. Johnston described Sankey's facial expression as "grim," while Lord Darling sat at Sankey's right, apparently with his eyes twinkling and lips twitching. Lord Tomlin sat next to Darling, while Lord Merrivale and Sir Lancelot Sanderson were on Sankey's left. "On the table before them are voluminous documents," wrote Johnston, "and legal papers, brought to them... by watchful attendants. Each of them has a glass of cold water beside him. The only ornaments on the table are three large silver ink-stands."

According to Johnston, Rowell stood at a little rostrum in the middle of the room to make his arguments.

A few members of the public, including half a dozen women, two or three bored-looking reporters, and a couple of ushers, make up most of those present.

It is all very orderly and dignified. Everyone is very polite. Mr. Rowell makes a statement, or reads long extracts from the BNA Act. Lord Merrivale, ponderous and very wise-looking, asks a question, and Mr. Rowell replies in many words.

Deep and intricate questions of constitutional law are debated back and forth. The exact shade of meaning to be placed on certain words is argued to the finest point.

And so it goes on, and probably will continue to go on for several days.

Johnston then sensibly concluded that, "at the end of all these endless speeches, lessons on Canadian history, and questions by five great judges of England, it will be decided, if one may hazard a guess, that women undoubtedly are Persons. Which one may say, without exaggeration, most of us know already!"[5]

The Decision Is Announced

Four days later, with all of the testimony heard, the court adjourned. While the judges weighed the evidence, everyone else with an interest in the case could only wait. And wait they did, for nearly three months.

Finally, on October 18, 1929, Lord Sankey, bewigged and dressed in a trailing robe, which a page carefully held above the pavement, walked to the Privy Council Chamber on Downing Street. He was preceded by two court officials, one carrying a mace, the other a coat of arms. He then broke from tradition by reading every page of the court's twenty-page decision, an indication that he fully recognized and appreciated the historical importance of the decision.

He minced no words when he explained that "the exclusion of women from all public offices is a relic of days more barbarous than ours." The fact that women had not traditionally held such public offices "is not of great weight." In Sankey's considered opinion, therefore, the BNA Act was not to be interpreted in the same context in which it had been written in 1867.

Sankey's decision included the following sentence, which is, incredibly, over 180 words in length.

> A heavy burden lies on an appellant who seeks to set aside a unanimous judgment of the Supreme Court, and this Board will only set aside such a decision after convincing argument and anxious consideration, but having regard: (1) To the object of the

Act—namely, to provide a constitution for Canada, a responsible and developing State; (2) that the word "person" is ambiguous, and may include members of either sex; (3) that there are sections in the Act above referred to which show that in some cases the word "person" must include females; (4) that in some sections the words "male persons" are expressly used when it is desired to confine the matter in issue to males; and (5) to the provisions of the Interpretation Act; their Lordships have come to the conclusion that the word "persons" in section 24 includes members both of the male and female sex, and that, therefore, the question propounded by the Governor General should be answered in the affirmative, and that women are eligible to be summoned to and become members of the Senate of Canada, and they will humbly advise His Majesty accordingly.

And then came the sentence that most pleased those five Alberta women. "The word 'person'... may include members of both sexes, and to those who ask why the word should include females, the obvious answer is why should it not?"

The decision of the Supreme Court of Canada had been reversed.

The ruling set a landmark legal precedent beyond the question of gender: it confirmed that the law must change with the times. Sankey explained that the British North America Act of 1867 was "planted in Canada, a living tree capable of growth and expansion within its natural limits." The ruling agreed with Justice Scott's decision more than a decade earlier, when Emily Murphy's role as judge was challenged, that the law must change with changing customs.

Of course Rowell was anxious to get the history-making good news to Emily as quickly as he could. For this verdict a telegram

A page carries the train of Chancellor John Sankey's robe
as the procession makes its way to Number One Downing Street,
the Privy Council, in London, England on October 18, 1929.
GLENBOW ARCHIVES NA-4953-1

simply would not do, so he phoned her from London. Because of
the time difference between the two cities, his call came at three in
the morning in Edmonton on October 19, 1929. Emily's daughter
Evelyn later described the scene this way: "Judge Murphy, in a
white flannelette nightgown, her hair tousled, her cheeks flushed,
was dancing with delight in the doorway. 'We've won! We've won.'"[6]

Once she had calmed down, Emily Murphy declared, on behalf
of her group of women, "It should be made clear that we, and the
women of Canada whom we had the high honour to represent, are
not considering the pronouncement of the Privy Council as standing for a sex victory, but, rather, as one which will now permit our
saying 'we' instead of 'you' in affairs of State."[7]

From Calgary, Nellie McClung told Murphy's hometown newspaper, the *Edmonton Journal*, "We are naturally elated, though

I must say we never despaired of ultimate victory. I am particularly glad for Mrs. Murphy's sake. It was she who wrote all the letters and arranged every detail in the controversy, assuming much of the expense and labour involved. Her handling of the whole matter has been a masterpiece of diplomacy and to her the victory belongs."

Henrietta Edwards optimistically predicted, "This decision marks the abolition of sex in politics."[8]

Families, neighbours, colleagues, and organizations were scrambling to host celebrations with the five victorious women as guests of honour. Newspapers across the country and internationally ran stories with headlines reading "Five Alberta Applicants Win Action," "Success in Canada May Influence Changes in the House of Lords," and "Canadian Women Beat Their English Sisters."

A dispute that had its roots in the complaints of a disgruntled local attorney in a courtroom on Canada's western frontier had made its way to the Privy Council Chamber in Downing Street in London, England, with all of its pomp and ceremony, wigs and gowns—but there it was. And finally the case was won.

The First Woman Senator

Women all across the country waited for Emily Murphy to be appointed to the Senate but, in keeping with his tradition, Prime Minister Mackenzie King waffled. He praised the victory but warned that "there are difficulties in the way which are insurmountable." Apparently those obstacles were not impediments to appointing forty-five-year-old Cairine Wilson, a Liberal supporter from Ontario, as the first woman senator in Canada in February 1930. By odd coincidence, Wilson was a distant relative of Henrietta Edwards.

The *Calgary Herald* reacted to the appointment with an editorial that read, in part, "It will be a matter of passing regret that the honour did not fall to a westerner. A group of Alberta women led the successful fight to assert the right of the sex to sit in the Senate."[9]

Cairine Wilson herself acknowledged the efforts of those Alberta women. She likely knew she was a much safer choice for that inaugural post than Emily Murphy would have been. Although historically overshadowed by the controversy of her appointment, Wilson served admirably as a senator until her death in 1960 at the age of seventy-five.

Perhaps no political or legal efforts would ever have been enough to allow Emily Murphy to realize her dream of becoming a senator, considering that a member of the Senate once exclaimed, "Oh, we could never have Mrs. Murphy as a Senator. She'd have made too much trouble, of course."[10] The man's assessment was likely correct, given that Emily herself often said, "Whenever I don't know whether to or not, I fight."[11]

The Aftermath

On October 29, 1929, only eleven days after Lord Sankey read his history-making decision, the New York City stock market crashed, heralding the economic chaos of the Great Depression, when mere survival was the only issue on the minds of many people. The horrors of the Second World War brought an end to the economic devastation of the Depression. And by the time the war was finally over in 1945, people were no longer concerned about archaic wordings of documents written in the 1800s or any possible consequences from them. They just wanted to get on with their lives. Women who had filled jobs vacated by soldiers when they left to fight overseas now returned to their homes, which were increasingly located in the peace and quiet of the city's suburbs.

Women were no longer preoccupied with fighting for their rights. They wanted to enjoy life, to have families and have some fun. Those early feminists were largely forgotten. They might have remained so if not for the women who are now referred to as Second Wave feminists, who in the 1960s and 1970s discovered the amazing stories of these women who had gone before them.

Lord Sankey's landmark ruling, which compared the British North America Act, Canada's constitution, to a "living tree," came to light again when Prime Minister Pierre Elliott Trudeau, signed the Proclamation of the Constitution Act in April 1982. The ceremony surrounding the signing took place on Parliament Hill in Ottawa, with Queen Elizabeth II looking on, and it marked the transfer of legislative authority from Great Britain to Canada. The Constitution Act, which includes the Charter of Rights and Freedoms, sets out Canada's system of government and protects the rights and freedoms of Canada's citizens. Since 1982 Canada's legal system, with the Supreme Court of Canada replacing the Judicial Committee of the Privy Council as the highest court, has continued to interpret and rule on the constitution and the Charter, showing that they are still a living tree, subject to growth and change.

CHAPTER
6

Later Years

Louise McKinney

The McKinneys were both active members of the Methodist Church. In 1925 when the Methodists merged with the Congregationalists and some Presbyterian congregations to become the United Church of Canada, Louise was the only female member of the Methodist Church to sign the agreement, and one of only four women in total to sign the document. The other signatories, all 346 of them, were men. Later she became commissioner of the first General Council of the United Church of Canada.

Louise was a popular and effective speaker who spent the rest of her life travelling throughout North America, Britain, and Europe to speak about reform, temperance, education, and women's rights.

Louise McKinney was a stalwart member of the Women's Christian Temperance Union. GLENBOW ARCHIVES NA 5395-4

She remained deeply involved with the Women's Christian Temperance Union and in 1931 was elected president of the Dominion WCTU. She also served as vice-president of the Imperial Order Daughters of the Empire (IODE).

In June 1931 she was named first vice-president of the World's Women's Christian Temperance Union. This took place at the organization's international convention in Toronto, which she hosted. Unfortunately, McKinney became ill while attending this conference. She died on July 10, 1931, a few weeks after returning home to Claresholm, Alberta. She was sixty-three years old.

Her death was noted in newspaper headlines, and tributes came from around the world. The WCTU national newsletter was filled with testimonials of respect. Representatives of the WCTU travelled from all across the country to attend McKinney's funeral, sitting in a group at the church service. At the graveside, each of these women placed a white ribbon on the coffin, their group's sign of purity and faith.

Willard, the McKinneys' only child, said of his mother, "She loved her work and valued her life as God's gift. She was content to accept the events of life as they came but at the same time did her utmost to make all things work together for good."

In Edmonton, Alberta's capital, Louise McKinney Park is located on the north shore of the North Saskatchewan River.

The province of Alberta recognizes McKinney's many contributions by offering Louise McKinney Scholarships for high-achieving students entering post-secondary education.

In 1937 Louise McKinney was recognized as a Person of National Historic Significance, and a plaque indicating that honour hangs in the Claresholm post office.

The people of Claresholm are still so proud of Louise McKinney that many tourism publications for the area include a short biography and description of her accomplishments.

Henrietta Muir Edwards

In August 1927 Henrietta Edwards happily accepted Emily Murphy's invitation and travelled from Fort Macleod to add her signature to those of Emily, Nellie McClung, Louise McKinney, and Irene Parlby on the letter that initiated the Persons Case. Because their names were alphabetized, the legal name of the case is *Edwards versus the Attorney General of Canada*. Although Henrietta never suggested that the impetus for the case was hers, Emily Murphy was known to have been annoyed when the older woman did not deny that such was the case. Coincidentally, when the subject of women senators arose, Edwards was often mentioned as an ideal candidate for the first appointment, but she was never nominated.

Later Years

In 1925 Henrietta's name was put forward to receive an honorary doctorate from the University of Alberta. The nomination was intended to recognize all she had accomplished for the province, but Henry Marshall Tory, the founding president of the university, felt that a woman recipient would be too controversial. (Some years later, Irene Parlby did receive an honorary doctorate from the university.)

Oliver, Henrietta's husband, died unexpectedly in 1915, and her daughter Margaret died in childbirth shortly after. Her son, Muir, one of the first four professors at the University of Alberta when it was founded in 1908, died ten years later, in 1918, while the university was closed during the worldwide influenza epidemic. Professor Edwards volunteered to nurse ailing students in a makeshift hospital on campus and, not surprisingly, contracted the fatal disease himself.[1]

Muir had purchased a home in Fort Macleod for his mother, who was in her seventies by then. Despite their privileged upbringing, Henrietta and her sister Amelia lived out their lives in that house under severe financial constraints. Henrietta seemed to accept her poverty as an important factor in her activism. In a speech to a women's group, she remarked:

Even more culpable than extravagance in cost... is the absolute slavery to fashion under which so many of us groan: a dress, a hat, a coat perfectly good in every way is discarded simply because it is last year's style... So many hours are spent in shopping, and exhausting conferences with dressmakers are held, all because fashion has ordered that sleeves must be no longer full at the wrist but full above the elbow. How far removed is such conduct from the actions of reasonable beings. What a simple waste of time, money and energy.[2]

On September 11, 1926, the day before Henrietta and Oliver would have celebrated their fiftieth wedding anniversary, she reflected with contentment on her life in a letter to her surviving daughter, Alice:

Fifty years ago this evening, I was married. If Oliver had been here we would have been celebrating our golden wedding. It seems impossible that that day which does not seem so very far back was fifty years ago.

In looking back the way seems strewn with blessings, hard places there were sometimes on the road but what happy companionship! What a son! What two dear daughters! What a husband! I think few women are as blessed as I. I feel grateful to God for I do not deserve what he has given me. My husband and I walked together in perfect accord for thirty-nine years. My children have never given me any anxiety. It is true I sit alone here tonight but Aunt Min is with me. In looking backward to childhood my path has been strewn with love and care, in looking forward is the joyful day of reunion.[3]

Henrietta Muir Edwards died on November 9, 1931, in Fort Macleod, Alberta. She was eighty-two years old. Henrietta is buried in Mount Pleasant Municipal Cemetery, Edmonton. Her epitaph reads, "Let her own works praise her. Her delight was in the law of the Lord."

Edwards was named a Person of National Historic Significance in 1962, and a plaque commemorating her contributions hangs in the Fort Macleod post office. The plaque, which was unveiled on July 18, 1964, reads, "A crusader for social and legislative reform, she devoted herself to these causes throughout her lifetime and was a member of 'The Group of Five' whose efforts led to recognition of women as persons eligible for appointment to the Senate of Canada, 1929." At the ceremony unveiling the plaque, a representative of the provincial government reminded the audience that Henrietta Muir Edwards was a leader of the suffragist movement in the West and strategic in the creation of the Alberta Dower Act of 1917.

Edwards is also remembered for having worked with Lady Aberdeen, Ishbel Hamilton-Gordon, wife of Canada's seventh Governor General, to establish the National Council of Women of Canada, the Victorian Order of Nurses, and the Young Women's Christian Association.[4]

In March 1981 Canada Post issued a Henrietta Muir Edwards commemorative stamp.

Henrietta Muir Edwards Park is on the south bank of the North Saskatchewan River in Edmonton, Alberta. Google honoured the 165th anniversary of her birth with a cartoon drawn by artist Kate Beaton.

Emily Murphy

Emily Murphy resigned from her history-making position as a magistrate in October 1931. She was sixty-three years old.

In her letter of resignation, addressed to the Attorney General of Alberta, she wrote that, "having served fifteen years as stipendiary magistrate in and for the City of Edmonton, and having passed the age period for retiring, it is now my desire to resign from this position," though if the AG approved, she offered to remain a police magistrate and judge of the juvenile court, "my services being available for relief work, or for any special duties such as you might require."

"It is with deep regret that I feel obliged to take this step," she wrote, "having been deeply interested in my work and in its various phases and having always received the utmost consideration from yourself and your predecessors in office."

The letter closed with an explanation that she planned to use her newly freed time "to finish a very considerable amount of literary work which is only partially written, and also to give a more personal attention to my own business affairs."[5]

Once she was retired from the courtroom, Emily Murphy usually spent her mornings working from bed where, according to her biographer, Byrne Hope Sanders, she had quite an efficient set-up for dealing with her voluminous correspondence. With the headboard of her bed softened by a layer of pillows, Emily wrote on a small wicker table perched on her lap. The sides of the table had pockets in which she kept the supplies she needed to have at hand—pens, pencils, envelopes, notepaper, and letters from people who needed or wanted her advice.

After lunch she might work in her garden, visit with a friend, or take the streetcar across the High Level Bridge and spend some time in downtown Edmonton. In the evenings, friends or neighbours often dropped in or the Murphys went out visiting. Although Arthur was in his mid-seventies by then, he was still in robust health and as active as ever. He never lost his love of sports or the outdoors.

On the morning of October 26, 1933, Emily appeared to be in good health. Her daughter Evelyn recalled that her mother had left the house earlier than usual and had taken the streetcar downtown, where she dropped in to the police station and the courthouse. There she sat in on the last case heard before the lunch hour. Many of her former colleagues were in the room. When Eardley Jackson, the Edmonton lawyer who originally raised the question of whether women were persons, saw Emily there, he announced, "Ladies and Gentlemen, we are honoured today by the presence of Mrs. Emily Murphy, Police Magistrate and Judge. A feminine note missing from this building is brought back by the kindly, smiling countenance of this beloved lady."[6] Murphy acknowledged the man's unexpected tribute with a smile and a nod. (Eardley Jackson had come to greatly respect his former foe, and for many years the two enjoyed a solid working relationship.)

While she was there she also visited with the cops on the beat. She always had a special fondness for those men—and they for her.

Then Emily walked to the public library. She intended to compile research material for an article denouncing Canada's latest upstart political party, the Canadian Commonwealth Federation. She did not think their policies were fair to Westerners. After a few hours at this, her eyes became tired because she had forgotten to bring her glasses. She phoned home and spoke to her daughter Evelyn, who agreed to drive the family car to fetch her mother. The two had plans to visit Emily's other daughter, Kathleen, who was married and had an adopted daughter, Emily Doris. Everyone in the family doted on the child, but especially the little girl's grandmother, perhaps because the child was Emily's namesake or, equally possibly, because Kathleen's daughter was also named for Emily's beloved daughter Doris, who had died of diphtheria three decades earlier.

Kathleen's house was under renovation, so she was not able to prepare a snack for her mother and sister. In keeping with Emily's taste for sweet baked goods, she and Evelyn stopped at a bakery and picked up a large bag of raisin buns for tea and to share with the men working on the renovation. The fact that the house was in a state of noisy chaos did not bother Emily at all. She always enjoyed being with her loved ones, and the sights and sounds of construction were nothing more than evidence of good honest labour.

Emily told her daughters that she and Arthur had recently made burial arrangements for themselves at the Edmonton Municipal Cemetery. This decision was a change, because previously they had always discussed "going back to Cookstown" for their place of eternal rest. By now, though, they had grown so fond of Western Canada that when the time came, they would prefer to be buried "under its wide skies."

Just before dinnertime that day, Emily and Evelyn drove the short distance back to the Murphys' home on 88th Avenue, just east of the University of Alberta campus. Arthur was at home by then, and the three of them ate dinner together. Afterward, Arthur went out for the evening. As he left the house, Evelyn remembered her mother teasing him about how young he still looked, and telling him that she hoped he had a good time at the basketball game he was planning to attend with his dear friend Bishop Burgett. They were going to watch the Edmonton Grads, an enormously popular women's basketball team that rarely lost a game—and ultimately set a North American record, which still stands, for the sports team with the best winning percentage.

By ten that evening, Emily went up to bed. Not long after, Evelyn brought her mother a warm drink. Evelyn teased Emily about the amount of cold cream on her face, only to be told, "Well, indeed, I'm not going to let myself get old and wrinkled!"

Evelyn turned out her mother's bedside lamp, gave her a kiss, and left the room. Once she was in her own room, Evelyn turned on the radio. She heard that, as expected, the Grads had won the game handily, and she called out the news to her mother, who was pleased to hear it.

After that, Evelyn recalled, "She must have gone right off to sleep, as she was sleeping when Dad got home. I told him not to go in and disturb her. I read in bed till about twelve and had just turned out the light when I heard one short cry."

Evelyn raced to her mother's room, but it was too late, for "she had left us." Arthur called the doctor, who was at Emily's side just a few minutes later, but he said she had died in her sleep. The little cry Evelyn heard was likely her body's last involuntary exhalation.

Although her death was completely unexpected and a terrible shock to the family, Evelyn later assured people that "she'd have wanted it. It was happy and free from all foreboding or sickness."

Emily Murphy was sixty-five years old when she died. The cause of death was officially given as a "cerebral emboli, with diabetes a contributing cause," although some suspected that she had died of a broken heart because, despite her heroic fight, in the end she was denied the Senate appointment she wanted so badly.

Emily's body lay in the living room of the family home, which was filled with floral tributes. A group of nuns visited, and members of the Salvation Army came, as did an assortment of policemen. Women who had once stood before Magistrate Murphy in her courtroom also came to pay their respects. One woman carried her child many blocks for the privilege of seeing her old friend one last time. Two other women, who had perhaps been brought into Emily's courtroom for soliciting, came bearing a single rose wrapped in newspaper. They placed it by Emily's hands, and the family left the flower there, knowing she would have wanted that.

Emily Murphy's funeral was held on October 30, 1933, at Holy Trinity Church, just a few blocks from her home. Her brother Gowan, her son-in-law Cleave Kenwood, and a handful of her favourite Edmonton policemen served as pallbearers. The mourners "lined the streets for blocks as her funeral cortege passed toward the church where the guard-of-honour from the city police stood at salute. They jammed the great church to its doors."[7]

Arthur, whom Emily had loved since she was sixteen; Gowan, her only remaining brother; daughters Kathleen and Evelyn; and Kathleen's husband saw Emily Murphy to her grave in Edmonton Municipal Cemetery.

Her tombstone reads:

Emily Ferguson Murphy ("Janey Canuck")
Beloved wife of Reverend Arthur Murphy, M.A.
Daughter of Isaac and Emily Ferguson
Born at Cookstown, Ontario, March 14, 1868
Died at Edmonton, Alberta, October 26, 1933

Later Years

Decorated by His Majesty King George V, A Lady of Grace
of the Order of St. John of Jerusalem in 1914.
First woman in the British Empire to be appointed a Police Mag-
istrate being also Judge of the Juvenile Court for the Province of
Alberta.
Originator and leader of the movement that admitted women to
the Senate of Canada.
Author, jurist, crusader in social reforms, great citizen.

"As when a standard bearer fainteth." Isaiah x, 18

Emily Murphy Park, located on the south side of the North
Saskatchewan River, just west of the University of Alberta campus,
is one of the most popular parks in the city of Edmonton. Two
plaques in the park acknowledge Murphy's contributions to Canadian history. One is at the base of a statue of Emily, which, like the
woman she was, is larger than life. It reads, in part,

Emily Ferguson Murphy, 'Janey Canuck,' a crusader for social
reform and for equal status for women, she devoted herself to
these causes with unremitting energy. Originator and leader of
the movement for the admission of women to membership in the
Senate of Canada, she became the first woman magistrate in the
British Commonwealth, Judge of the Edmonton Juvenile Court.

Another plaque, placed on August 17, 1960, almost thirty-three
years after she wrote her history-making letter to the federal government, was unveiled by the City of Edmonton Archives and

Landmarks Committee, women's organizations and many friends. It reads:

> This memorial in honour of Emily Ferguson Murphy.
>   Well known for her warm humanity and for her public service which brought her recognition throughout Canada.

Emily Murphy Road runs adjacent to the park.

Emily was deemed a Person of National Historic Significance in 1958. A chapter of the Imperial Order Daughters of the Empire is known as the Emily Murphy Chapter because the group wished "to be known by the name of a woman who is representative of the finest in achievement for her sex."

Murphy's Home

Emily Murphy's house, where the five women gathered on August 27, 1927, for their groundbreaking meeting, still stands. The property at 11011 88 Avenue in Edmonton is now owned by the University of Alberta. It stands just east of the main campus and currently houses Student Legal Services. The house is listed on the Canadian Register of Historic People and Places.

Newton Rowell

In May 1938 Newton Rowell suffered a heart attack and, some weeks later, a stroke. Life can be sadly ironic, and this was certainly the case for Rowell, as the stroke stripped him of his ability to speak, the very skill that had helped make his career, and for that matter his life, a success. Rowell died on November 22, 1941, in Toronto. He was seventy-four years old.

Later Years

Nellie McClung

Nellie McClung was the best-known member of the Famous Five, even eclipsing Emily Murphy, the group's leader. In the 1930s, the McClungs moved to Victoria, BC, where Nellie continued to write and tour, promoting her books and, equally fervently, the fight against social injustice.

Nellie became an elder with her church, the first woman to do so in Canada. She was the only woman delegate at the 1938 League of Nations convention in Geneva, Switzerland.

Prime Minister Mackenzie King and Nellie McClung never lost their admiration for one another, and in 1936 he appointed her to the first board of directors of the newly created Canadian Broadcasting Corporation. She found the board meetings a trial, not only because they required travel from Vancouver Island to Ottawa, but also because her fellow board members were, she felt, all stodgy old men. Despite these irritations, she dedicated herself to the position until suffering a heart attack at a CBC meeting. After that she could no longer deny that her health was failing, and she finally scaled back her activities.

Nellie McClung died on September 1, 1951. She was seventy-eight years old. Her death made headlines across the country, and her funeral had to be held at a large church in downtown Victoria because her home parish could not accommodate all the mourners who came to pay their respects.

Nellie is buried in Royal Oak Burial Park, just north of Victoria. Her grave is marked with the words "Loved and Remembered."

Popular historian Grant MacEwan, the former mayor of Calgary and lieutenant-governor of Alberta, noted that Nellie McClung was a woman of extraordinary energy and determination, and that she "demanded some useful accomplishment from every day."[8]

In 1957 the Women's Institute in Grey County, Ontario, where Nellie was born, erected a cairn at her birthplace.

In 1954 Nellie McClung was named a Person of National Historic Significance.

The Nellie McClung branch of the Greater Victoria Public Library system is located on Cedar Hill Road in Victoria. Nellie McClung Park is south of the North Saskatchewan River, near Queen Elizabeth Park in Edmonton. Nellie McClung Collegiate is located in Manitou, Manitoba, and Nellie McClung Public School is in Vaughan, Ontario. The Nellie McClung Charter School is an all-girls program within Edmonton Public Schools.

Irene Parlby

By the 1930s, Irene Parlby had clearly become adept at the game of politics. She worked diligently as a politician, often in conjunction with fellow representative Nellie McClung, to bring about improvements in the lives of women, especially rural women. She was honoured to accept when Prime Minster Robert Bennett appointed her as one of three delegates to represent Canada at the 1930 League of Nations conference in Geneva.

In 1935 Parlby gave a speech entitled "What Business Do Women Have in Politics?" In it she reflected, "I never realized until my first campaign in 1921 what miserable incompetent creatures women were in the eyes of the public. I ought to have developed a terrible inferiority complex by the time it was over for practically the only issue that seemed to concern the electorate or the opposition, was that I was a woman and worse, an English woman at that, who although she had been in the country from 1896 when the country was still an undeveloped wilderness, could not possibly know anything about Canada."[9]

Parlby declined to run for office again in the 1935 election. Perhaps she understood that the voters' loyalties had shifted. When the ballots were counted, the Social Credit Party had swept the province, electing William Aberhart as premier and leaving the UFA without a seat in the legislature.

Irene Parlby served for many years on the board of governors of the University of Alberta. At spring convocation in 1935, she was granted an honorary doctorate from that institution, the first woman ever to receive this distinction, although Henrietta Muir Edwards had been suggested for an honorary degree ten years before.

January 9, 1965, was Irene's last birthday. She turned ninety-seven, and the occasion was celebrated with bouquets of flowers from the UFWA as well as cards and letters from admirers all across Canada. She died on July 12 of that year. She was the last surviving member of the Famous Five and is buried in the Alix cemetery. The Parlbys' descendants continue to live in that area of central Alberta as well-respected citizens.

Parlby once threatened to make a bonfire of all the official papers she had accumulated during her political career and then dance merrily beside the flames. Author Nancy Millar speculates that perhaps Parlby actually did that, because her archival fonds "are much slimmer than the ones for the other of the Famous Five."[10]

Parlby was the only rural member of the Famous Five. In 1966 she was named a Person of National Historic Significance.

A plaque commemorating Parlby's contributions hangs in the post office in Alix, Alberta.

Irene Parlby Park in Edmonton is located on the bank of the North Saskatchewan River at the Low Level Bridge.

7

Looking Back

HISTORY IS ALWAYS played out within the social context of the time. The Roaring Twenties, when the Persons Case was working its way through to the top of the court system, was a unique era. The horrors of the Great War and the worldwide influenza epidemic were in the past, and the Great Depression had not yet become a gruelling reality. People were partying. Flappers were flapping. Speakeasies were quenching the thirsts brought on by long, dry periods of prohibition. Canada's population was booming. The economy was flourishing as never before, with unprecedented industrial growth. By then the sight of automobiles on the roads no longer terrorized people. Instead, it seemed that everyone wanted to own one. This gave birth to an entirely new service industry, one in which many people made a great deal of money. Charlie Trudeau, the father of one future prime minister and the grandfather of another, was one of those people. He made his fortune in service stations.

Historian Jack Granatstein described it as being "the best of times." He acknowledged that, for women, "the decade was one of gain." In the 1920s, women's organizations, such as the Women's Christian Temperance Union (WCTU), Women's Institutes, and the National Council of Women of Canada (NCWC), were still thriving, and with so many members having the right to vote, the groups had become significant political forces. Henrietta Edwards, Nellie McClung, Louise McKinney, Irene Parlby, and Emily Murphy were in leadership roles, and all five women were popular and powerful. Their achievements, individually and collectively, were recognized and applauded internationally.

They also had their detractors, however, who saw their doctrines as stridently racist and exclusive. As well, their staunch insistence on temperance was losing popularity.

Eugenics

The women who made up the Famous Five lived in times of great social change.

During the 1800s, scientific discoveries and inventions were revolutionizing the way people lived, worked, and thought. Suddenly anything was possible, or so it seemed. Science was hailed as the world's great saviour. With better knowledge of nutrition, people would be stronger and healthier, and would live longer. With the invention of work-saving machines, the production of goods increased, sparking economic growth worldwide.

In 1883 scientist Francis Galton, a cousin of Charles Darwin, introduced a new school of scientific investigation called "eugenics."

Looking Back

The word is derived from a Greek term meaning "well born," and theorists in the field implied that prudent breeding could improve the quality of the human race, while weeding out less desirable characteristics. The standards for desirable criteria were set by upper- and middle-class white Christians. And so the eugenics movement, which is, effectively, mandated racism, was born.

Many Canadian women's groups, including the WCTU, the NCWC, and some chapters of the UFWA, dedicated themselves wholeheartedly to promoting the eugenics movement. The members believed that Canada's burgeoning population growth was to blame for what they saw as a deterioration in the quality of Canadians. And eugenics would keep the white race dominant. As distasteful as that philosophy sounds today, the premise was taken even further, to include sterilization, voluntary or involuntary, of those deemed to be carrying less-than-desirable genes.

All five of the women who would come to be called the Famous Five were staunch supporters of eugenics.

Emily Murphy, in her position as a judge, was of course exposed to a daily parade of criminals. She declared in the *Winnipeg Tribune* that "feeble minded" or "insane" people made up four percent of the country's population. It's unclear where her statistic came from. She reasoned that forbidding such people from having children would improve the calibre of Canadian citizens.

Irene Parlby used her position as a member of Alberta's legislative assembly to warn citizens that with "insane" or "mentally deficient" people reproducing, society was in serious jeopardy. The only way to stop that threat was to sterilize those deemed to be unfit.

Nellie McClung was equally outspoken, writing in one of her syndicated newspaper columns about neighbours whose daughter was thought to be "mentally defective." This family, McClung attested, suffered endless disruptions due to the girl's behaviour until she was surgically sterilized. After that, all was peace and harmony in the home.

The movement gained followers, and on March 7, 1928, the Alberta Sexual Sterilization Act was passed and a Eugenics Board was created. From that date until 1972, when the act was finally repealed, nearly three thousand people were sterilized in Alberta, many against their will. British Columbia passed a similar act but was not as rigorous in its application, although there is no way to get exact numbers of sterilizations, as the province's records have been destroyed. And, of course, eugenics in the guise of "racial cleansing" became a fatal reality in parts of Europe, Germany specifically.

Alcohol and Illegal Drugs

On a hot day in July 1915, Emily Murphy and Nellie McClung led a procession of some twelve hundred temperance supporters along Edmonton's main thoroughfare. The group, mostly women, was determined to have the sale of alcohol banned, at least in the province of Alberta. Their demonstration was successful, and the following year Alberta became a dry province. Although the local marchers' efforts were significant, their protest coincided with the First World War, when all grain and fruit crops were needed for food rather than alcohol, which helped bring about prohibition.

By the end of the war, people were anxious to leave enforced austerity behind. Temperance had little place in the Roaring Twenties, and by the mid-1920s, buying alcohol was legal once more. Early in May 1924, on the same stretch of road where Emily and

Looking Back

Nellie had led their fellow teetotalers less than ten years earlier, "Six Men and a Dog" waited in line for a liquor store to open. The first sale recorded in that store was to a woman who bought six bottles of stout.[1] Members of the WCTU, Emily Murphy and Nellie McClung included, had lost their battle, but they did not give up the fight.

Emily had a front-row seat to observe the carnage alcohol and drug abuse inflicted on individuals and families. She blamed much of the drug trade on the recent wave of immigration, especially the Chinese men who had been brought to Canada to build the railway. While there is no denying that the Chinese workers brought opium with them, it is unscientific—and racist—to blame them as the sole reason illegal drugs were introduced and available.

Magistrate Murphy was so concerned about the problem that for the first time she wrote and published a book under her own name, rather than her nom de plume. *The Black Candle* did not become the bestseller that Emily's Janey Canuck books had been. Those were collections of pleasant anecdotes that people, especially women, enjoyed reading. *The Black Candle* was not intended for a general audience but was aimed at bureaucracies and government policy makers. As such, it had a worldwide impact that lasted for generations to come.

Murphy wrote about the dangers of drug use and the drug trade, claiming that immigrants were corrupting white Christian morals. She predicted that if the situation were left unchecked, the British Empire's domination was at risk. Despite her efforts to exhaustively research the topic, her data was subjective at best.

Copies of *The Black Candle* were sent to the League of Nations and from there distributed to all member nations. Every level of government in Canada, as well as police departments across Canada and the United States, adopted the book as a reference. Emily Murphy was in great demand as a public speaker. She travelled extensively to spread her anti-drug doctrine. She even nominated herself and her book for the Nobel Prize in 1923.[2] Although her bid for that coveted award failed, many Canadian newspapers and periodicals reviewed the work positively, indicating that it contained important information that people needed to have, and the book influenced drug laws for decades.[3]

Now such harsh and racist views are offensive, but they were very much the norm when *The Black Candle* was first published in 1922. While Nellie, Emily, Irene, Henrietta, and Louise had revolutionary views on women's rights, they were often not able to see beyond the accepted views of their day on race.

CHAPTER

8

The Famous Five

SOMETIME AFTER LORD SANKEY'S decision, Emily Murphy commented that the battle "took thirteen years and nearly broke my heart."[1] But in hindsight, any battle that ends with jubilant, middle-of-the-night shouts of glee—"We've won! We've won!"—has to have been worth the effort.

Many years after the Privy Council victory, Emily's daughter Evelyn, who acted as her secretary during the years of the struggle, wrote to a friend, "I must say it riles me when they talk of the 'Famous Five' when all the other four women did was allow their names to stand with mother's in her appeal to the Privy Council. She did all the rest on her own. I know because I typed the letters. The four others only lent their names to one petition but paid none of the costs, nor did any of the work in taking the case through the different courts. But now they are the 'Famous Five.' It's really funny."[2]

Evelyn's irritation is no doubt drawn from a daughter's love and pride in her mother's accomplishments. And it is unclear how or when exactly Emily Murphy, Henrietta Muir Edwards, Nellie McClung, Louise McKinney, and Irene Parlby came to be collectively known as the Famous Five. The name dates back at least to the 1930s. There are also references to them as the Alberta Five and, occasionally, the Valiant Five. In French, the women are known as Célèbres Cinq.

Commemorations

Since 1979, the fiftieth anniversary of the Privy Council's decision that women are indeed "persons," October 18 has been known as "Persons Day" in Canada. That year, the government of Canada instituted the Governor General's Awards in Commemoration of the Persons Case, which are awarded each year to recognize women who have made significant contributions to women's equality. To date, over two hundred prizes have been awarded.

Also that year, the Alberta government established Persons Case Scholarships to celebrate the victory of the five women who had made Alberta their home. These awards are intended for high-achieving female post-secondary students who are enrolled in fields that are traditionally male dominated, or whose studies "will advance gender equality and promote the self-advocacy of women."[3]

The Persons Case was recognized as a National Historic Event in 1997. A plaque commemorating that recognition is located in Emily Murphy Park in her hometown of Edmonton, Alberta.

On October 18, 1999, seventy years after the Famous Five's victory, a statue by sculptor Barbara Patterson, featuring Emily

Murphy, Henrietta Edwards, Nellie McClung, Louise McKinney, and Irene Parlby celebrating their win, was unveiled in Calgary's Olympic Park.

The impetus for this tribute came from a group of five women in Calgary who, in 1996, formed the Famous 5 Foundation to honour the original five women while encouraging today's women to continue to fight for gender equality. The installation was funded with donations solicited by the foundation's members.

A year later an identical installation was unveiled on Parliament Hill. It is one of the most visited sites on the Hill.

In 2004 the Canadian mint issued a fifty-dollar bill honouring the Famous Five.

On October 12, 2009, almost exactly eighty years after Lord Sankey presented his decision in the Persons Case, Henrietta Muir Edwards, Nellie McClung, Louise McKinney, Irene Parlby, and Emily Murphy were made honorary senators. Of course, by then Emily Murphy had been dead for more than seventy-five years, so was no longer a threat to the peace and comfort of the Senate chambers.

Frances Wright, the founder of the Famous 5 Foundation, said of the posthumous appointments, "It's a fabulous gift. It shows that dreams in Canada can come true and particularly when you dedicate your life ... to contributing to the growth of Canada."[4]

In Winnipeg, sculptor Helen Granger Young's statue of the five women stands on the grounds of the Manitoba legislature. It was commissioned by the Nellie McClung Foundation and was unveiled on June 18, 2010.

In July 2012 a mural of the Five, painted by artist Kris Friesen, was unveiled at 10027 102 Street in downtown Edmonton.

Women Senators

In February 1930 four months after Lord Sankey's ruling, Liberal prime minister William Lyon Mackenzie King appointed Cairine Wilson to the Senate, the first woman to sit in the Red Chamber. Since then there have been ninety-four women senators. The first from Alberta was Martha Bielish, appointed by Prime Minister Joe Clark in 1979.

A Commemorative Plaque in the Senate Foyer

On June 11, 1938, the Association of Business and Professional Women of Canada presented a brass plaque to be placed in the Senate foyer honouring the Famous Five. Only Nellie McClung attended the unveiling. Emily Murphy, Henrietta Muir Edwards, and Louise McKinney had died by that time. Irene Parlby, who was seventy years old, chose not to leave her rural Alberta home for the occasion.[5]

The plaque reads: "To further the cause of womankind, these five outstanding pioneer women caused steps to be taken resulting in the recognition by the Privy Council of women as persons eligible for appointment to the Senate of Canada."

At the presentation, Nellie McClung looked resplendent in an evening gown and new shoes that she later admitted pinched her feet. The mutual admiration of Prime Minister William Lyon Mackenzie King and Nellie McClung was as evident as ever. Now that Emily Murphy had died and was no longer a threat with her ambitions to become a senator, the prime minister praised the persistence of the women who made up the Famous Five. Nellie then took the podium and responded with her usual warmth, wit, and humour:

I thank the Prime Minister... for the kindness he showed to our little petition when it was just a little scrap of paper going around and not very welcome any place. I also wish to thank Newton Wesley Rowell for his kindness in taking our petition to the Privy Council and I also wish to thank Lord Sankey for his glorious decision, so clear cut and unmistakable and unanswerable. [laughter from the audience]

I would very much like tonight, my dear friends, if I could express the minds, not only of the five of us, but of all people who have advanced the cause of women by means seen and unseen. The great unnumbered and unremembered and unknown people who have done so much for us, the people whose names will never appear in the paper, the people whose names we'll never know, because it has been a long task, it has been an epic story, this rise of women. They had to begin from so far down. Women had first to convince the world that they had souls and then that they had minds and then it came along to this political entity. [more laughter from the audience] And the end is not yet. We feel that there are still people who would sign the minority report. Now I wish to pay my tribute of love and admiration to the other four women whose friendship I enjoyed and treasured, for their loyalty and for their love and steadfastness, for their wonderful companionship. Mrs. McKinney, Mrs. Muir Edwards, and Mrs. Parlby... and particularly I wish to give my tribute of praise to our undaunted and indomitable and incomparable leader, Emily

The Famous Five's victory in the Persons Case is commemorated
with statues in Ottawa, Calgary, Edmonton and this one on
the grounds of the Manitoba Legislature in Winnipeg.
GOVERNMENT OF MANITOBA, COPYRIGHT OFFICE,
ON BEHALF OF THE QUEEN'S PRINTER OF MANITOBA

F. Murphy. She didn't care who got the honour. She was never
one to care who got the vote of thanks. She would joyfully pin
a medal anytime on somebody else, and you know dear friends,
I can't help but saying now that we're all here together that we
would all be able to accomplish a great deal more if none of us
cared who got the credit, and tonight if she is listening from some
other [of] the islands of bliss, I'm sure that there is no person
who will hear the words of this ceremony with a lighter and a
merrier heart.

The Famous Five

When Nellie McClung returned to her Vancouver Island home after the ceremony in Ottawa, she wrote a newspaper column for national syndication that would draw attention to the amazing accomplishments of her friend Emily Murphy. Nellie began, "Everything in life is a circle. There are no sharp corners. Cause and effect run together all the way. The event that took place a week ago in Ottawa, when a plaque was unveiled commemorating the decision of the Privy Council that women are persons, was a culmination of something that began twenty years ago in the Women's Court in Edmonton."[6]

She reminded readers of the origins of the case in Eardley Jackson's challenge of Murphy's right to sit as a magistrate, noting that

> Murphy, being a wise woman, looked carefully into the matter. She often said that one must never belittle the argument of the opponent. She read the famous case of Charlton vs. Ling on 1868 and its ruling: "Women are not persons in matters of rights and privileges, but they are persons in matters of pains and penalties." The law had not been rescinded, and there was no doubt that it was still valid, though public opinion had rendered it obsolete.

Nellie then describes the slow process of lobbying politicians, who lamented that it "would take time and careful thought" to amend the BNA Act. However, "Murphy, whose business it was to know the law, believed that there was a way of getting this matter cleared up. We would ask the Parliament of Canada for an interpretation of this clause."

Nellie brings to life the day in August 1927 when she and the other four women gathered at Emily Murphy's home in Edmonton to sign the petition. She describes the Supreme Court decision that "came as a shattering blow to our hopes."

> In the opinion of the Supreme Court of Canada, women were not persons!
>
> Four out of the five judges based their judgment on the common-law disability of women to hold public office, and the other one believed the word 'person' in the BNA Act meant male person, because the framers of the act had only men in mind when the clause was written.
>
> We met again, this time in Calgary, and contemplated our defeat. Murphy was still undaunted. We would appeal the Supreme Court decision. We would send our petition to the Privy Council.
>
> We asked her what we would use for money. Lawyers' fees, we knew were staggering. When a lawyer is writing his fees for a service of this kind, his hand often slips. Murphy said she would write to the prime minister. Perhaps he could devise a way. This was every woman's concern and she was sure that the government would be glad to have it settled.

And then she tells of Lord Sankey's decision that "was so simple and plain that we wonder now why we did not think of it ourselves." According to Nellie, the Judicial Committee of the Privy Council "found the solution in the British North America Act itself, under two headings":

> First: There are clauses in the act where the word 'male' persons is used, which leads one to believe that 'person' must mean male and female person.

Second: There is one clause in the act where the word 'person' must mean male and female. It is Clause 133, which provides that either the French or English language may be used by any persons in any court established under this act. The word 'person' must include women, as it is inconceivable that this privilege was given to men only.

There were other reasons given in His Lordship's fourteen-page judgment, but that was the one that closed the debate.

Now it is over. The circle is complete. The Business and Professional Women of Canada have graciously placed a memorial plaque in the lobby of the Senate, House of Parliament, Ottawa, to mark this event. The speeches will be over when this appears in print.

There are only two of us left now of the five, and we feel, as did Mrs. Edwards and Mrs. McKinney, that we, like all women of Canada, are indebted to Emily. F. Murphy for this definite, clear-cut victory, which has clarified the position of women in the whole British Empire.

The Famous Five, with Emily Murphy as their strong and unquestioned leader, fought for the women of Canada, but also the women of the world.

Timeline

1834 Lower Canada prohibits women from voting because of the potential for "dangerous conditions" at polling stations.

1843 New Brunswick declares that women are prohibited from voting.

1849 Henrietta Muir (Edwards) is born in Montreal, Quebec.

1867 The British North America Act (BNA Act) is signed and becomes the constitution of the Dominion of Canada, which consists of New Brunswick, Nova Scotia, Quebec, and Ontario. Section 41 of the BNA Act declares that "every Male British Subject, aged Twenty-one Years or upwards, being a Householder, shall have a Vote."

1868 Emily Ferguson (Murphy) is born in Cookstown, Ontario.

Irene Marryat (Parlby) is born in England.

Louise Crummy (McKinney) is born in Frankville, Ontario.

1870 Prince Edward Island, Manitoba, and British Columbia join Confederation.

1873 Nellie Mooney (McClung) is born in Chatsworth, Ontario.

Female property owners in British Columbia are granted the right to vote in municipal elections.

1874 Henrietta Muir and her sister Amelia establish the forerunner to the Young Women's Christian Association.

1875 Henrietta Muir publishes a newsletter for working women.

1876 Henrietta Muir marries Dr. Oliver Cromwell Edwards.

Timeline

The Toronto Women's Literary Club is formed by Dr. Emily Stowe, Canada's first woman doctor. The title of the organization is purposely deceitful, allowing the members to work toward suffrage undetected.

1880 Nellie Mooney moves with her family to the Souris Valley, Manitoba.

1882 Unmarried female property owners are granted the right to vote in Ontario's municipal elections.

1883 Henrietta Muir Edwards moves with her family to Indian Head (in what is now Saskatchewan).

The Toronto Women's Literary Club changes its name to the Toronto Suffrage Association.

1885 The Last Spike of the Canadian Pacific Railway is ceremoniously pounded into the ground, officially linking Canada from coast to coast.

1887 Emily Ferguson marries Arthur Murphy.

Manitoba grants women property holders the right to vote in municipal elections.

Toronto Suffrage Association becomes a national organization.

1889 Nellie McClung takes a teaching job in Manitou, Manitoba.

1890 Henrietta Muir Edwards's husband becomes ill, and the family moves back to Montreal and later to Ottawa.

The Women's Christian Temperance Union (WCTU) in Manitoba merges with a group of Icelandic women who had formed a suffragist league some years before.

1893 Henrietta Muir Edwards, in conjunction with Lady Aberdeen, wife of the Governor General, organizes the National Council of Women of Canada and is appointed to lead the organization's Standing Committee on Laws. She maintains that post for the rest of her life.

Louise Crummy takes a job teaching in North Dakota and joins the WCTU.

1894 Women in New Brunswick form the Women's Enfranchisement Association.

The Equal Suffrage Club is formed in Manitoba. After successful debates, petitions, and rallies, the matter of women's suffrage is ready to be presented to Manitoba's Provincial Assembly, but the item is left off the agenda and never sees the light of day.

In Ottawa, the House of Commons votes against a petition from the WCTU for women's suffrage.

1896 Nellie Mooney marries Wes McClung.

Louise Crummy marries James McKinney.

1897 Irene Parlby moves to Canada.

Henrietta Muir Edwards, along with Lady Aberdeen, forms the Victorian Order of Nurses.

1898 The Murphy family moves to England.

Irene Marryat marries Walter Parlby.

1900 Murphy family returns to Canada and lives in Toronto, Ontario.

1901 Emily Murphy's first book, *Impressions of Janey Canuck*, published.

1903 Murphy family moves to Swan River, Manitoba.

Henrietta Muir Edwards and her family move back to the Canadian west.

Louise McKinney and her family move to Claresholm, Alberta. Louise starts a local chapter of the WCTU. Within a year there are twenty chapters of the organization in western Canada.

1905 Alberta and Saskatchewan become provinces.

1907 Murphy family moves to Edmonton, Alberta.

Louise McKinney becomes vice-president of the WCTU and represents Canada at the group's World Conference in Boston, Massachusetts.

1908 Nellie McClung's first book, *Sowing Seeds in Danny*, is published.

1909 The United Farmers of Alberta (UFA) is formed. The organization goes on to become a political party.

Henrietta Muir Edwards is a delegate to the National Council of Women of Canada conference.

1910 Emily Murphy's second book, *Janey Canuck in the West,* is published.

The Married Women's Relief Act is passed in Alberta.

National Council of Women of Canada officially endorses women's suffrage.

1911 The McClung family moves to Winnipeg, and Nellie McClung becomes an activist for women and children.

Timeline

1912 Emily Murphy's third book, *Open Trails*, is published.

Winnipeg Political Equality League is formed with the support of the WCTU and the Manitoba Grain Growers.

Saskatchewan Grain Growers petition the government to enfranchise women.

1913 Emily Murphy becomes president of the Canadian Women's Press Club.

Louise McKinney represents Canada at the WCTU's world conference in Brooklyn, New York.

1914 Emily Murphy takes on the vice-presidency of the National Council of Women of Canada.

Emily Murphy's fourth book, *Seeds of Pine*, is published.

Nellie McClung and her colleagues present a mock parliament in Winnipeg to highlight the absurdity of women not having the vote.

"The shots heard around the world" are fired, killing Archduke Franz Ferdinand of Austria and his wife, and leading to the start of the First World War.

The McClung family moves to Edmonton, Alberta.

1915 Nellie McClung's second book, *In Times Like These*, is published.

The Saskatchewan Homestead Act is passed.

Alberta Married Women's Home Protection Act is passed.

In Saskatchewan, the Provincial Equal Franchise Board is formed. The legislature is too busy with other "exceedingly important matters" to deal with the petition, signed by ten thousand petitioners, presented by the Franchise Board.

Helen MacMurchy is appointed in Ontario as the "inspector of the feeble minded." She influenced the National Council of Women of Canada to accept a policy of sterilization of "defective" people.

1916 Voting rights are granted to some women in Manitoba, Saskatchewan, and Alberta.

Emily Murphy becomes the first woman in the British Empire to be appointed a police magistrate and, subsequently, judge of children's court.

Emily Murphy is challenged on her right to serve as a judge because, under the BNA Act, women are not considered "persons."

Justice Scott of the Alberta Supreme Court rules that women are "persons."

Irene Parlby becomes first president of Alberta's United Farm Women's Association.

1917 Voting rights are granted to some women in Ontario and British Columbia.

Henrietta Muir Edwards's book *Legal Status of Women in Canada* is published by the federal government.

Louise McKinney is the first woman legislator in the British Empire.

The Dower Act of Alberta is passed, granting property rights to women in Alberta.

1918 The right to vote in provincial elections is granted to some women in Nova Scotia.

The right to vote in federal elections is granted to some Canadian women over the age of 21.

First World War ends.

Manitoba's Dower Act is passed, guaranteeing a wife's inheritance and right of veto.

1919 The right to vote in provincial elections is granted to some women in New Brunswick.

Some Canadian women are granted the right to run in federal elections.

Emily Murphy's name is put forward as a candidate for the Senate, but the wording of the BNA Act dictates that she's not a person and therefore is not qualified.

1920 Irene Parlby is appointed to the University of Alberta Board of Governors.

Louise McKinney represents Canada at the WCTU's conference in London, England.

1921 Mary Ellen Smith is appointed Minister Without Portfolio in British Columbia's Liberal government. She is the first woman in the British Empire to be a cabinet minister.

Nellie McClung is elected in Alberta as a Liberal member of the legislative assembly (MLA).

Irene Parlby is elected in Alberta as an MLA with the UFA and is appointed Minister Without Portfolio. She becomes the second woman in the British Empire to be a cabinet minister.

Timeline

Agnes Macphail is the first woman elected to the House of Commons.

1922 Voting rights are granted to some women in Prince Edward Island.

Emily Murphy's fifth book, *The Black Candle*, her first without the nom de plume Janey Canuck, is published.

1924 Emily Murphy takes a leave from her responsibilities in the courts to accept Prime Minister Mackenzie King's request that she attend the 1924 League of Nations Conference in Geneva, Switzerland.

1925 Voting rights are granted to some women in Newfoundland, which does not join Confederation until 1949.

As Minister Without Portfolio, Irene Parlby sponsors the Minimum Wage for Women Act.

1926 Nellie McClung is defeated by a slim margin in her bid to win a second term as a provincial MLA.

Irene Parlby is re-elected as an MLA.

1927 Emily Murphy invites Henrietta Muir Edwards, Nellie McClung, Louise McKinney, and Irene Parlby to co-sign her letter to the Supreme Court of Canada requesting clarification on the interpretation of the word "persons" in the BNA Act.

1928 The Supreme Court decides that under the terms of the BNA Act, women are not to be considered "persons."

The five women cannot accept that decision and send a petition to the Privy Council in England.

Louise McKinney represents Canada at the WCTU conference in Lausanne, Switzerland.

1929 On October 18, the Privy Council rules that Canadian women are "persons."

Emily Murphy's name is unsuccessfully put forward for a seat in the Senate.

1930 Cairine Wilson becomes the first woman in the Canadian Senate.

Irene Parlby is elected for a third term as MLA.

Prime Minster Robert Bennett appoints Irene Parlby as one of three delegates to represent Canada at the 1930 League of Nations conference in Geneva, Switzerland.

1931 Emily Murphy retires as judge.

Henrietta Muir Edwards dies.

Louise McKinney becomes first vice-president of the World's Women's Christian Temperance Union.

Louise McKinney dies.

1933 Emily Murphy dies.

Nellie McClung and her husband move to Vancouver Island.

1935 Nellie McClung's autobiography is published.

Irene Parlby is awarded an honorary doctorate from the University of Alberta.

1936 The Canadian Broadcasting Corporation is formed. Prime Minister William Lyon Mackenzie King appoints Nellie McClung to the board of directors. She is the only woman on the board.

1938 Nellie McClung represents Canada at the League of Nations conference in Geneva, Switzerland.

Nellie McClung is the only member of the Famous Five to be on Parliament Hill for a ceremony unveiling a plaque honouring the women's successful fight to be recognized as "persons." The plaque still hangs near the Senate chambers.

1940 Voting rights are granted to some women in Quebec.

1945 Part two of Nellie McClung's autobiography, *The Stream Runs Fast,* is published.

1948 Canadian citizens of Asian descent are granted the right to vote.

1950 Inuit people gain the right to vote in federal elections, but polling stations are inaccessible to them until 1962.

1951 Nellie McClung dies.

Indigenous people gain the right to vote.

1960 Indigenous people gain the right to vote without jeopardizing their Indian status.

1965 Irene Parlby dies.

Acknowledgements

THANK YOU TO Rodger Touchie, publisher of Heritage House, for so enthusiastically embracing the idea of this book. Thank you to Lara Kordic. Warmest thanks to Audrey McClellan.

Thank you to the people of Alix Wagon Wheel Museum, the Claresholm Museum, the Fort Macleod Archives, the Famous 5 Foundation, the Nellie McClung Foundation, the National Council of Women of Canada, the Glenbow Archives, the Provincial Archives of Alberta, the City of Edmonton Archives, the United Church of Canada Archives, the Vancouver Island Regional Library, the Greater Victoria Public Library, and the Toronto Public Library.

I am enormously grateful to the researchers and writers who have gone before me. Your work has helped me and informed this book, but any mistakes between the covers are my own.

Thank you to my daughters and niece for saying "yes" when I asked them to take photos during Alberta's long, cold winter.

Thank you to booksellers everywhere.

Thank you to my family and friends for their support.

Thank you to Bob. Your unconditional love means the world to me.

Notes

Prologue

1. Syndicated weekly newspaper column from June 18, 1938, reprinted in Barbara Smith, ed., *The Valiant Nellie McClung*, 129.
2. This recipe is from Christine Mander, *Emily Murphy, Rebel*, 144.

Chapter 1: Who Were These Women?

1. The first two chapter titles in Robert J. Sharpe and Patricia I. McMahon's book, *The Persons Case*, are "The First of the Five" (about Emily Murphy) and "The Other Four." See also Nancy Millar, *The Famous Five*, 9.
2. The main sources of information about each of the women and the Persons Case itself are listed in the Bibliographical Essay at the end of the book.
3. National Council of Women of Canada, *Women of Canada: Their Life and Work* (1900). There is a digitized version of this book at the Early Canadiana Online website, eco.canadiana.ca/view/oocihm.11965/ 17?r=0&s=1.
4. Nellie described this encounter with Wes in the first volume of her autobiography, *Clearing in the West*.
5. Quoted in Millar, *The Famous Five*, 83–85.
6. Quoted in ibid., 94.
7. Quoted in ibid., 95.
8. Donna James, *Emily Murphy*, 5.
9. Ibid., 12.
10. Quoted in Byrne Hope Sanders, *Emily Murphy, Crusader*, 96.

Chapter 2: Working Together (The 1910s)

1. Kym Bird, "Mock Parliament, 1914," Canadian Encyclopedia website, thecanadianencyclopedia.ca/en/article/mock-parliament-1914.
2. Moushumi Chakrabarty, "Amelia Yeomans," Canadian Encyclopedia website, thecanadianencyclopedia.ca/en/article/amelia-yeomans.

Notes

3. Ibid.
4. Linda Rasmussen, Lorna Rasmussen, Candace Savage, Anne Wheeler, *A Harvest Yet to Reap: A History of Prairie Women*, 174.
5. Quoted in Margaret Macpherson, *Nellie McClung: A Voice for the Voiceless*, 90.
6. "Alice Jane Jukes Jamieson," on the Alberta Champions website, albertachampions.org/Champions/alice-jane-jukes-jamieson-1860-1949/.
7. Alice Jamieson is featured on the Jamieson Place website, jamiesonplace. com/index.php/amenities-services/alberta-champions.
8. "Alice Jamieson Girls' Academy," brochure from the Calgary Board of Education, cbe.ab.ca/programs/program-options/teaching-philosophy/ Documents/Alice-Jamieson-Girls-Academy-Brochure.pdf.
9. Rasmussen et al., *A Harvest Yet to Reap*, 148.
10. Information on similar acts passed throughout Canada can be found on the Nellie McClung Foundation website, ournellie.com/learn/ womens-suffrage/canadian-history-of-womens-rights/.
11. Quoted in David G. Bettison, John K. Kenward, and Larrie Taylor, "The Past and the Generation of Basic Issues, 1880 to 1935," in *Urban Affairs in Alberta*, 26.
12. See Nancy Millar, *The Famous Five*, 66, and "Henrietta Muir Edwards" on the Wineglass Ranch website, wineglassranch.ca/family-heritage/ henrietta-muir-edwards. The Wineglass Ranch, originally in southern Alberta, was established by Henrietta's daughter and son-in-law, Alice and Claude Gardiner. Their great-grandchildren re-established the ranch in the Peace River country in the 1990s, and have extensive information on their ancestors on the website.
13. Quoted in Elaine Leslau Silverman; updated by Susanna Mcleod, "Henrietta Edwards," Canadian Encyclopedia website, thecanadianencyclopedia.ca/en/article/henrietta-louise-edwards.
14. Quoted in Grant MacEwan, *And Mighty Women Too*, 30.
15. Elaine Leslau Silverman; updated by Susanna Mcleod, "Louise McKinney," Canadian Encyclopedia website, thecanadianencyclopedia. ca/en/article/louise-mckinney.
16. Debbie Culbertson, "Roberta MacAdams Price," Canadian Encyclopedia website, thecanadianencyclopedia.ca/en/article/roberta-macadams-price.

17. Quoted in Millar, *The Famous Five*, 95.

18. MacEwan, *And Mighty Women Too*, 146.

19. Catherine Cavanaugh and Susanna Mcleod, "Irene Parlby," Canadian Encyclopedia website, thecanadianencyclopedia.ca/en/article/ mary-irene-parlby.

20. Quoted in Millar, *The Famous Five*, 97.

21. Cavanaugh and McLeod, "Irene Parlby."

22. Article in *The Grain Growers' Guide*, December 4, 1918; quoted in MacEwan, *And Mighty Women Too*, 153.

23. All three messages are quoted in Christine Mander, *Emily Murphy: Rebel*, 94.

24. Quoted in Byrne Hope Sanders, *Emily Murphy, Crusader*, 142.

25. Quoted in Millar, *The Famous Five*, 17.

26. MacEwan, *And Mighty Women Too*, 136.

27. Quoted in Sanders, *Emily Murphy, Crusader*, 216.

Chapter 3: The Political Battle (1917 to 1927)

1. Quoted in Byrne Hope Sanders, *Emily Murphy, Crusader*, 217.

2. Charlotte Mander, *Emily Murphy, Rebel*, 96.

3. Nancy Millar, *The Famous Five*, 34.

4. Quoted in Sanders, *Emily Murphy, Crusader*, 217.

5. Quoted in ibid., 79.

6. Sanders, *Emily Murphy, Crusader*, 220–22.

7. Robert J. Sharpe and Patricia I. McMahon, *The Persons Case*, 79.

8. Sanders, *Emily Murphy, Crusader*, 216.

9. Nellie McClung, *Firing the Heather*, 208; Sharpe and McMahon, *The Persons Case*, 88.

10. Quoted in Sanders, *Emily Murphy Crusader*, 218.

11. Donna James, *Emily Murphy*, 51.

12. McClung, *Firing the Heather*, 208.

13. Parliament of Canada website, lop.parl.ca/sites/ParlInfo/default/ en_CA/People/Profile?personId=4800#comp; Wikipedia, s.v. "Daniel Edward Riley," last modified September 3, 2018, en.wikipedia.org/wiki/ Daniel_Edward_Riley.

14. McClung, *Firing the Heather*, 209.

15. Robert J. Sharpe and Patricia I. McMahon, *The Persons Case*, 221n20.

Notes

16. Quoted in Robert J. Sharpe and Patricia I. McMahon, *The Persons Case*, 106.

Chapter 4: The Legal Battle (1927 to 1929)

1. Quoted in Robert J. Sharpe and Patricia I. McMahon, *The Persons Case*, 106. A commonly held belief regarding the Persons Case states that Emily Murphy's brother, William Ferguson, drew her attention to a statement in Section 60 of the Supreme Court Act, reading, "any five interested parties could petition for an order-in-council directing the Supreme Court to rule on a constitutional point in the British North America Act." But in their book *The Persons Case*, Robert J. Sharpe and Patricia I. McMahon state, "*The Supreme Court Act* did not allow for petitions of this kind and there has never been such a procedure." They add that neither Emily nor her brother was behind the fiction. In her December 1932 letter to Mrs. J.P. Hynes, the publicity convener for the Federated Women's Institutes, Murphy acknowledged, "It was not necessary that five persons be named as Appellants."
2. All three quotes are from Byrne Hope Sanders, *Emily Murphy, Crusader*, 222.
3. Sharpe and McMahon, *The Persons Case*, 185.
4. Sanders, *Emily Murphy, Crusader*, 238.
5. Quoted in Nancy Millar, *The Famous Five*, 47.
6. Quoted in Sanders, *Emily Murphy, Crusader*, 237, 238.
7. Catherine Cleverdon, *The Women's Suffrage Movement in Canada*, 144.
8. Quoted in Sanders, *Emily Murphy, Crusader*, 238.

Chapter 5: The Judicial Committee of the Privy Council (1928 to 1929)

1. Quoted in Bryn Hope Sanders, *Emily Murphy, Crusader*, 239.
2. Quoted in Robert J. Sharpe and Patricia I. McMahon, *The Persons Case*, 139.
3. Quoted in Sanders, *Emily Murphy, Crusader*, 241.
4. Quoted in Sharpe and McMahon, *The Persons Case*, 178.
5. Johnston's article is quoted in Byrne Hope Sanders, *Emily Murphy, Crusader*, 243, 244.
6. Quoted in Sanders, *Emily Murphy, Crusader*, 249.
7. Ibid., 251.

8. McClung and Edwards quotes from Charlotte Mander, *Emily Murphy, Rebel*, 125.
9. Quoted in ibid., 126.
10. Ibid.
11. Quoted in Nancy Millar, *The Famous Five*, 9.

Chapter 6: Later Years

1. "Remembering the Service and Sacrifice of William Muir Edwards," *Folio* (University of Alberta online newsletter), November 13, 2013, folio.ca/remembering-the-service-and-sacrifice-of-william-muir-edwards/.
2. Quoted in Nancy Millar, *The Famous Five*, 69.
3. Ibid., 70.
4. Robert J. Sharpe and Patricia I. McMahon, *The Persons Case*, 38, 39.
5. Quoted in Byrne Hope Sanders, *Emily Murphy, Crusader*, 333.
6. Ibid., 336, 337.
7. Ibid., 340.
8. Grant MacEwan, *And Mighty Women Too*, 160.
9. Quoted in Sharpe and McMahon, *The Persons Case*, 53–54.
10. Millar, *The Famous Five*, 97.

Chapter 7: Looking Back

1. Reported in the *Edmonton Journal* of May 12, 1924.
2. Robert J. Sharpe and Patricia I. McMahon, *The Persons Case*, 30.
3. Byrne Hope Sanders, *Emily Murphy, Crusader*, 209.

Chapter 8: The Famous Five

1. Donna James, *Emily Murphy*, 76.
2. Quoted in Nancy Millar, *The Famous Five*, 9.
3. "Persons Case Scholarships," on the Alberta Student Aid website, studentaid.alberta.ca/scholarships/alberta-scholarships/?sK=219 (accessed January 30, 2019).
4. Quoted in Jennifer Yang, "'Famous Five' Named Honorary Senators," *Toronto Star*, October 12, 2009.
5. This description of the event draws on the account in the *Edmonton Bulletin*, May 4, 1930.
6. Syndicated weekly newspaper column from June 18, 1938, reprinted in Barbara Smith, ed., *The Valiant Nellie McClung*, 129–30.

Bibliographical
Essay and References

Emily Murphy and the Persons Case

The information presented here about Emily Murphy's life and times was gleaned from a number of sources. And because Emily was the driving force behind the Persons Case, many of the sources that were particularly helpful for researching her life were also crucial sources of information about the political and legal battle. *The Canadian Encyclopedia* (Hurtig Publishers, 1988), both online and original, was a go-to for fact checking throughout the project.

In 1945 Macmillan Canada in Toronto published *Emily Murphy, Crusader*, by Byrne Hope Sanders, long-time editor of Chatelaine magazine. Although certainly dated in its writing style, this book was an invaluable resource.

Fitzhenry and Whiteside produced a line of books called The Canadians. Donna James wrote *Emily Murphy* for this series. It is a slim book, only sixty-four pages, but includes more than thirty archival photographs and is an excellent summary of Emily's life, as is Christine Mander's 1985 work, *Emily Murphy, Rebel*, published by Simon and Pierre, Toronto. Susan Jackel wrote Emily's biography for the Canadian Encyclopedia online, with updates by Catherine Cavanaugh and Tabitha Marshall (thecanadianencyclopedia. ca/en/article/emily-murphy).

Robert J. Sharpe and Patricia I. McMahon's book *The Persons Case: The Origins and Legacy of the Fight for Legal Personhood* was published in 2007 by the University of Toronto Press for The Osgoode Society for Canadian Legal History (it was reprinted in 2008). Both Sharpe and McMahon are lawyers and, as the book's title implies, their work is focused on the legal aspects of the case, but it is accessibly written and gives excellent background on all the women.

Nancy Millar, a Calgary author devoted to Canadian social history, wrote and published *The Famous Five: Five Canadian Women and Their Fight to Become Persons* in 1999. The book does a thorough job of covering the topic and the women's lives. Like the Sharpe and McMahon book, Millar justifiably highlights Emily Murphy's life. The archival photographs are well chosen to bring the subject to life.

In 1975 Grant MacEwan, author, local historian, and former lieutenant-governor of Alberta, published a book of short biographies about Alberta pioneers entitled *Fifty Mighty Men*. That work was followed quickly by *And Mighty Women Too*. Here he includes short biographies of all five women—and forty-five other "notable western Canadian women."

A Harvest Yet to Reap: A History of Prairie Women, by Linda Rasmussen, Lorna Rasmussen, Candace Savage, and Anne Wheeler, was a project of Alberta Education, funded by the Alberta Heritage Savings Trust Fund. Although published in 1979, the book remains a gold mine of information, illustrations, and photographs for anyone interested in Western Canadian women's history.

Websites from several women's organizations, including the Famous 5 Foundation and the Nellie McClung Foundation, were also very helpful.

Bibliographical Essay and References

Henrietta Edwards

Information about Henrietta Edwards's life is available from the Fort Macleod Museum and Archives, the Women's Christian Temperance Union, and the Federated Women's Institutes of Canada. Elaine Leslau Silverman and Susanna Mcleod wrote Henrietta's biography for the Canadian Encyclopedia online (thecanadian encyclopedia.ca/en/article/henrietta-louise-edwards).

The Wineglass Ranch, originally in southern Alberta, was established by Henrietta's daughter and son-in-law, Alice and Claude Gardiner. Their great-grandchildren re-established the ranch in the Peace River country in the 1990s, and have extensive information on their ancestors on the ranch website, including examples of Henrietta's artwork (wineglassranch.ca/index.php).

Nancy Millar's book *The Famous Five* contains a chapter about Henrietta, with some excellent photographs. Robert J. Sharpe and Patricia I. McMahon's *The Persons Case* also includes an informative section about Edwards.

The Provincial Archives of Alberta in Edmonton and the Glenbow Archives in Calgary are excellent and useful sources of information about and photographs of Henrietta Edwards. The Famous 5 Foundation's website is another good resource, as is the National Council of Women of Canada. A digitized version of the NCWC's book *Women of Canada: Their Life and Work* from 1900, with two chapters by Henrietta, is available at the Early Canadiana Online website (eco.canadiana.ca/view/oocihm.11965/17?r=0&s=1).

Nellie McClung

Nellie McClung wrote two autobiographies. The first, *Clearing in the West*, was published by Thomas Allen in 1935, while the second,

The Stream Runs Fast, came from the same publisher ten years later. Scholars Veronica Strong-Boag and Michelle Lynn Rosa combined the two biographies in *The Complete Autobiography of Nellie McClung,* which came out in 2003. There is no doubt that Nellie herself would have been pleased with the women's work, which is both scholarly and enjoyable to read.

No Small Legacy: Canada's Nellie McClung, Blazing a Trail for Faith and Justice, by Carol L. Hancock, published in 1986 is an especially useful resource concerning, but not limited to, Nellie McClung's church affiliations. *Nellie McClung,* by Mary Lile Benham, is part of Fitzhenry and Whiteside's The Canadians series. It is a slim book but gives a thorough review of McClung's life with excellent context.

Mary Hallett and Marilyn Davis wrote an excellent book about Nellie McClung, *Firing the Heather: The Life and Times of Nellie McClung,* in 1993. *Nellie McClung: A Voice for the Voiceless,* by Margaret Macpherson, is another informative source. And my own book *The Valiant Nellie McClung, Selected Writings By Canada's Most Famous Suffragist,* contains an assortment of Nellie's weekly syndicated columns as well as a brief biography.

The Nellie McClung Foundation and its website have been so helpful to me while researching this book and also when I was compiling *The Valiant Nellie McClung* in 2016.

Mary E. Hallett wrote Nellie's biography for the Canadian Encyclopedia online (thecanadianencyclopedia.ca/en/article/nellie-letitia-mcclung) and Kym Bird wrote about the mock parliament in Winnipeg in 1914 for the encyclopedia (thecanadianencyclopedia.ca/en/article/mock-parliament-1914). Both articles include the Heritage

Minute about Nellie McClung, which includes a staged excerpt from her speech at the mock parliament. Nellie McClung is also the only member of the Famous Five (so far) who has been included in the Dictionary of Canadian Biography Online (biographi.ca/en/bio/mooney_helen_letitia_18E.html). Her biography there was written by Michelle Swann and Veronica Strong-Boag.

Louise McKinney

The Claresholm Museum is a good resource for information about Louise McKinney, as are the Women's Christian Temperance Union website and the Methodist Church archives. The Federated Women's Institutes of Canada and the Canadian National Council of Women also have informative websites and are very responsive to queries.

Both Nancy Millar's book, *The Famous Five*, and Sharpe and McMahon's book, *The Person's Case,* devote sections to Louise McKinney's life and contributions.

Elaine Leslau Silverman and Susanna Mcleod wrote Louise's biography for the Canadian Encyclopedia website (thecanadian encyclopedia.ca/en/article/louise-mckinney).

Irene Parlby

The Alix Wagon Wheel Museum in Alix, Alberta, is an excellent resource for information about the Parlbys, and the people at the museum are extremely helpful. The Provincial Archives of Alberta in Edmonton and the Glenbow Museum in Calgary hold photographs and text relating to Irene Parlby, and records from the Alberta Legislature offer information on her years of service as a cabinet minister.

The Persons Case, by Robert J. Sharpe and Patricia I. McMahon, includes an informative section on Irene Parlby, as does Nancy Millar's book *The Famous Five*.

Catherine Cavanaugh and Susanna McLeod wrote Irene's biography for the Canadian Encyclopedia website (thecanadian encyclopedia.ca/en/article/mary-irene-parlby).

Bibliography

Benham, Mary Lile. *Nellie McClung*. The Canadians Series. Markham, ON: Fitzhenry and Whiteside, 1975.

Bettison, David, John K. Kenward, and Larrie Taylor. *Urban Affairs in Alberta*. Edmonton: University of Alberta Press, 1975.

Bothwell, Robert, and J.L. Granatstein. *Our Century: The Canadian Journey*. Toronto: McArthur and Company, 2000.

Christensen, Jo-Anne, and Dennis Shappka. *An Edmonton Album: Glimpses of the Way We Were*. Toronto: Hounslow Press, 1999.

Cleverdon, Catherine. *The Women's Suffrage Movement in Canada*. Toronto: University of Toronto Press, 1950 (reprinted 1975).

Hallett, Mary, and Marilyn Davis. *Firing the Heather: The Life and Times of Nellie McClung*. Saskatoon: Fifth House, 1993.

Hancock, Carol L. *No Small Legacy: Canada's Nellie McClung, Blazing a Trail for Faith and Justice*. Winfield, BC: Wood Lake Books, 1986.

James, Donna. *Emily Murphy*. The Canadians Series. Markham, ON: Fitzhenry and Whiteside, 2001.

MacEwan, Grant. *And Mighty Women Too: Stories of Western Pioneers*. Vancouver: Greystone Books, 1995.

Macpherson, Margaret. *Nellie McClung: A Voice for the Voiceless*. Montreal: XYZ Publishing, 2003.

Mander, Charlotte. *Emily Murphy: Rebel*. Toronto: Simon and Pierre, 1985.

Millar, Nancy. *The Famous Five: Five Canadian Women and Their Fight to Become Persons*. Calgary: Deadwood Publishing, 2003.

Rasmussen, Linda, Lorna Rasmussen, and Candace Savage. *A Harvest Yet to Reap: A History of Prairie Women*. Toronto: The Women's Press, 1979.

Rollans, Scott, and Ken Davis. *The Albertans*. Edmonton: Lone Pine Publishing, 1981 (reprinted 2005).

Bibliographical Essay and References

Sanders, Byrne Hope. *Emily Murphy, Crusader*. Toronto: Macmillan, 1945.

Sharpe, Robert J., and Patricia I. McMahon. *The Persons Case: The Origins and Legacy of the Fight for Legal Personhood*. Toronto: University of Toronto Press, 2008.

Smith, Barbara, ed. *The Valiant Nellie McClung: Selected Writings by Canada's Most Famous Suffragist*. Victoria: Heritage House, 2016.

Strong-Boag, Veronica, and Michelle Lynn Rosa, eds. *Nellie McClung: The Complete Autobiography*. Peterborough, ON: Broadview Press, 2003.

Books by the Famous Five

Emily Murphy

The Impressions of Janey Canuck Abroad (1901)
Janey Canuck in the West (1910)
Open Trails (1912)
Seeds of Pine (1914)
The Black Candle (1922)
Bishop Bompas (1929)

Nellie McClung

Sowing Seeds in Danny (1908)
The Second Chance (1910)
The Black Creek Stopping House (1912)
In Times Like These (1915, reprinted 1975)
The Next of Kin (1917)
Three Times and Out (1917)
Purple Springs (1921)
When Christmas Crossed the Peace (1923)
Painted Fires (1925)
All We Like Sheep (1930)
Be Good to Yourself (1930)
Flowers for the Living (1931)
Clearing in the West: My Own Story (1935)
Leaves from Lantern Lane (1936)
More Leaves from Lantern Lane (1937)
The Stream Runs Fast: My Own Story (1945)

BARBARA SMITH

Henrietta Muir Edwards
Legal Status of Canadian Women (1908)
Legal Status of Women in Alberta (1921)

Index

Index

About the Author

BARBARA SMITH WAS born and raised in Toronto and lived most of her life in Edmonton, before settling in the Victoria area in 2006. She is a full-time author whose work is inspired by a lifelong interest in social history, combined with a love of mystery. Smith has published over thirty books, most of which are collections of ghost stories  inspired by true events, including *Campfire Stories of Western Canada*, *Ghostly Campfire Stories of Western Canada*, *Great Canadian Ghost Stories*, and perennial bestsellers *Ghost Stories of Alberta*, *Ghost Stories and Mysterious Creatures of British Columbia*, and *Ghost Stories of the Rocky Mountains*. She was also featured on the Discovery Channel's *Hunt for the Mad Trapper*. She lives in Sidney, BC.